# I'm Here

## A PEER COUNSELING GUIDE FOR TEENS

James J. Crist, Ph.D., C.S.A.C.

art by
Jomike Tejido

free spirit
PUBLISHING®

**Library of Congress Cataloging-in-Publication Data**
Names: Crist, James J., author.
Title: I'm here : a peer counseling guide for teens / James J. Crist, Ph.D., C.S.A.
Description: Minneapolis, MN : Free Spirit Publishing, an imprint of Teacher
    Created Materials, [2024] | Includes bibliographical references and index. |
    Audience: Ages 11+
Identifiers: LCCN 2024003374 (print) | LCCN 2024003375 (ebook) | ISBN
    9798885543767 (paperback) | ISBN 9798885543774 (ebook) | ISBN
    9798885543781 (epub)
Subjects: LCSH: Peer counseling--Juvenile literature. | Teenagers--Mental
    health--Juvenile literature. | Adolescent psychology--Juvenile literature. |
    BISAC: YOUNG ADULT NONFICTION / Health & Daily Living / Mental
    Health | YOUNG ADULT NONFICTION / Social Topics / Emotions & Feelings
Classification: LCC BF636.7.P44 C75 2024  (print) | LCC BF636.7.P44 (ebook) |
    DDC 371.4/047--dc23/eng/20240216
LC record available at https://lccn.loc.gov/2024003374
LC ebook record available at https://lccn.loc.gov/2024003375

Edited by Cassie Labriola-Sitzman
Design by Colleen Pidel
Cover art and illustrations by Jomike Tejido

Printed by: 70548
Printed in: China
PO#: 11570

**Free Spirit Publishing**
An imprint of Teacher Created Materials
9850 51st Avenue North, Suite 100
Minneapolis, MN 55442
(612) 338-2068
help4kids@freespirit.com
freespirit.com

FSC
www.fsc.org
MIX
Paper | Supporting
responsible forestry
FSC® C144853

## Dedication

I would like to dedicate this book to all the kids and teens I have worked with in counseling over the years. Many times you have told me that you used the strategies I taught you to help your friends deal with their problems. These stories helped inspire this book, which I hope will in turn inspire many more kids and teens to help each other and make the world a better place.

## Acknowledgments

I would like to thank Kyra Ostendorf at Free Spirit for reaching out to me with the idea for writing this book. I'd like to thank my editor, Cassie Labriola-Sitzman, for her wonderful suggestions and edits. Finally, I would like to thank Judy Galbraith, founder of Free Spirit Publishing, for believing in me when I first started writing for Free Spirit back in 2004 and for developing a staff that has always been a pleasure to work with. Finally, I would like to thank Jomike Tejido for his wonderful cover art and illustrations and for giving the book a friendly vibe.

# CONTENTS

# Introduction

As a professional therapist, I've spent my career working with young people. I've listened as teens talk about feelings and problems in their lives. I've helped them come up with solutions. And I've taught them strategies they can use to deal with their problems and improve their relationships. But the skills I've used in this work didn't grow overnight. I had to learn them first, and then I practiced them, over and over again, on my own and with my clients. A few things have stood out to me during this time. Mainly, that respect for another person's ideas and thoughts, along with an understanding of their feelings, is key to being able to help them. Being a good listener comes in handy too!

It's not only counselors and therapists like me who listen to people's feelings and problems and help them find solutions. People show up for one another in this way every day. Families and neighbors support each other through challenges big and small. Friends help each other navigate the ups and downs of life, school, and growing up. Peers can make school a nightmare or a safe haven. Many of the kids and teens I've worked with have told me that they shared the suggestions I gave them with friends, near and far, who are going through similar problems.

These kind and supportive people fill an important role. The reality is that there are not enough licensed counselors and therapists to serve everyone who needs them. And this lack is keenly felt in schools—more so since the start of the Covid-19 pandemic. During the worst of the pandemic, when most schools were shut down and doing virtual learning, many kids and teens suffered from lack of or reduced contact with friends. Learning became more difficult and more frustrating. Other stressors, such as families not having enough money to pay bills, caregivers losing their jobs, social and political issues, worries about the climate crisis and other environmental issues, and concerns about being able to find a good job after finishing school, weighed even more heavily. When schools needed more counselors, there weren't enough. And those who were available became harder to reach. Even with the pandemic closures officially over, the stresses kids and teens are facing have not let up. And there still aren't enough counselors to go around.

Schools around the world have used peer counseling to try to fill this gap. They train students to become peer counselors who help other students at their schools struggling with a variety of problems. But you don't have to be a designated peer counselor to do this. Anyone can learn strategies and skills for talking with friends and peers. In fact, many kids and teens talk to each other about their frustrations, often before they reach out to adults or trained helpers, if they reach out at all.

# About This Book

It can be stressful if a friend talks to you about their problems. You might feel good that they trust you enough to share with you, and you want to help . . . but you're not sure what you can say or do. And you definitely don't want to make things worse! That's where this book comes in.

Many of the skills that professional counselors learn and that young people are taught in peer counseling programs can be used by anyone. My goal is to share some of these skills, as well as some of the knowledge I've gained over the years, so you can support the people in your life. Because when a person has someone to talk with, someone who will listen and offer a sympathetic ear and who can help them figure out how to cope and come up with solutions to problems, this makes all the difference in the world. So, if you want to learn how you can help your friends, family members, and classmates when they come to you with problems and how you can be part of making your school and community a kinder, safer, and more welcoming place, this book is for you!

# How to Use This Book

By reading this book, you can learn many valuable skills that will help you know what to do when people come to you with problems. In the chapters that follow, I share basic helping skills, including listening and asking questions. I also share strategies for helping people come up with solutions to problems, set goals, and work through conflict, as well as advice for what to do if someone needs more help than you can give.

Some of the information in this book applies mostly to trained peer counselors or other formal peer helpers. (Chapters 2 and 3, as well as the Peer Counselor Tips throughout, are specifically geared toward this audience, but are valuable for everyone to learn.) But most of the strategies can be used by anyone who wants to learn how to help in an informal way. By learning these skills and putting them into practice, you might even decide that you want to help start a peer counseling program at your school!

Try reading the book all the way through first to get a feel for the various strategies that you might use when someone comes to you for help. You can go back to specific chapters or sections as situations arise. As you read, think about how the skills might help you in your own life too. And if, after reading the book and practicing the skills, you think you might want to choose to help others as a career, that would be awesome!

## CHAPTER 1

# Teens Helping Teens

**Maria:** "You look a bit down today. What's up?"

**Jordan:** "I haven't been getting along with my parents lately."

**Maria:** "Sorry to hear that. How so?"

**Jordan:** "Well, they're always on me about my grades. It's really stressing me out!"

**Maria:** "I can relate to that. What have you tried so far to deal with it?"

This conversation is one that might take place on the bus, in a school hallway, between members of a team or club, at an after-school program, at home, in a peer counseling office—or anywhere young people meet and spend time together. And it's a good example of how people your age can support one another.

In this chapter, you'll learn about mental health problems and stressors young people face, how you can help friends and peers formally and informally, the various helping roles you can take, the advantages of helping, where you can offer help, and how you can be a part of anti-bullying efforts at your school.

# The Increase in Mental Health Problems

Mental health and addiction problems have increased significantly in recent years, including among young people. The problem is so serious that in 2021 a national emergency in child and adolescent mental health was declared in the United States by the American Academy of Pediatrics, the American Academy of Child and Adolescent Psychiatry, and the Children's Hospital Association.

The most recent data from the US Centers for Disease Control and Prevention (CDC) estimates that ADHD, anxiety, behavior problems, and depression are the most common mental disorders in children and

## RATES OF COMMON MENTAL HEALTH DISORDERS IN KIDS AND TEENS

- 9.8% (about 6 million) have ADHD
- 9.4% (about 5.8 million) have an anxiety disorder
- 8.9% (about 5.5 million) have behavior problems
- 4.4% (about 2.7 million) have depression

(CDC 2023)

teens. Nearly 22 percent of kids and teens have one or more diagnosable mental health disorders. That is about one in every five kids.

Depression, suicide, and substance abuse are also important concerns among teens. The US Department of Health and Human Services reported that in 2021, one out of every five teens had severe depression during the previous year. Of those, almost 75 percent had symptoms that interfered with their ability to do well at school or work, complete their chores at home, get along with family members, or have a social life. Over half of these kids did not receive any kind of treatment. Chances are that you or someone you know has had at least some trouble handling the stresses of daily life.

## RATES OF DEPRESSION, SUICIDE, AND SUBSTANCE ABUSE IN TEENS

- 36.7% have had persistent feelings of sadness or hopelessness
- 15.1% have had a major depressive episode
- 4.1% have a substance use disorder
- 1.6% have an alcohol use disorder
- 3.2% have an illicit drug use disorder
- 18.8% have seriously considered attempting suicide
- 15.7% have made a suicide plan
- 8.9% have attempted suicide
- 2.5% have made a suicide attempt requiring medical treatment

(CDC 2023)

Alcohol and drug use are also common among teens, and among some middle schoolers. According to the CDC's 2021 Youth Risk Behavior Survey, almost 60 percent of high school seniors had tried alcohol at least once. About 30 percent had used in the last 30 days. Over one-third (36.8 percent) had used marijuana at least once, and 21.7 percent had used in the last 30 days. Often, people turn to drugs or alcohol to handle situations or emotions that feel overwhelming. But some drugs, such as heroin, fentanyl, or prescription drugs, can be deadly if the user overdoses. People can also die from drinking too much alcohol. While not all teens who use alcohol and drugs have problems as a result, using these substances can make mental and physical health problems and social problems worse.

## Causes of Stress Among Kids and Teens

Growing up can be pretty stressful. Trying to juggle keeping up with friends, getting good grades, meeting family obligations, working part-time, participating in sports or clubs, and thinking about your future can get overwhelming. Such stresses are perfectly normal and usually get better with time as you mature and are better able to handle them.

Situations or problems such as divorce or other family issues, bullying, being unhoused, dealing with food insecurity, and having trouble with learning are longer term types of stress. They can often make life harder and are much more difficult to cope with than everyday stressors. Traumatic events such as assault, domestic violence, and physical or sexual abuse can take a long time to overcome. When these problems persist over long periods of time, they can affect your mental and physical health.

Young people everywhere have experienced a great deal of stress and trauma in recent years. And high levels of stress can make people more vulnerable to developing mental health or addiction problems. Issues around the Covid-19 pandemic, in particular, have contributed to an increase in mental health problems and addictions in teens and adults.

Racism, intolerance, and hate crimes are challenging and stressful issues that many kids and teens face. Violence based on race and religious beliefs has risen, making young people from targeted communities feel unsafe. Experiences of racial discrimination and the trauma resulting from them can contribute to physical symptoms and mental health issues such as depression, anxiety, substance use, and post-traumatic stress disorder (PTSD). They can even cause damage to the brain.

Discrimination and violence on the basis of gender identity and sexual orientation have also worsened in recent years. LGBTQ+ teens continue to face extremely high levels of violence and mental health challenges. The CDC's 2021 Youth Risk Behavior Survey found that half of LGBTQ+ high school students reported having poor mental health and more than one in five (22 percent) had attempted suicide in the past year. Laws are being passed in many places to make it harder for people, and especially young trans people, to receive gender-affirming care.

Traditional gender role expectations are another source of stress for many. Though times are changing, many boys are still afraid to talk about and express their feelings out of fear that doing so is a sign of weakness. This can make it difficult for them to ask for help when they need it and may explain why suicide rates are higher for boys and men than other gender groups. Girls also face pressure based on gender. Sexual harassment, being treated as less capable or less competent, and being called degrading names can harm their self-esteem. It can be hard for girls to tell others if they have been a victim of harassment or assault, because many fear that no one will believe them.

All these issues have led to increased stress in young people and an increased need for professional mental health help. Even so, there are still not enough mental health and addiction professionals available.

# How Young People Can Help One Another

While, as a young person, you are not expected to fill the role of a professional, there are many informal ways you can help friends, family members, and peers.

Talking with people about their feelings or problems and offering support is one way to help. Not all kids and teens feel comfortable talking with adults about their problems. Some may worry about being lectured or judged. Talking about risky behaviors can also lead to consequences. Admitting you smoke marijuana to a teacher or school counselor might result in disciplinary action. Talking with a friend or peer can feel easier and safer. For many young people, just talking about a problem can help them feel better and less alone, even if there isn't a clear solution.

You can also help when you see someone being bullied. You might step in and try to defuse the situation or find an adult if you think someone is in danger of being hurt. You can ask, "Hey, what's going on?" as you walk toward the person being bullied. You can also help by telling people to "knock it off," inviting the person being bullied to walk away with you, checking in on them, or offering to help them report the bullying.

If you see a classmate sitting by themselves, this might be another opportunity to help. You could introduce yourself and ask if they'd like some company. You could invite them to join you and your friends. Befriending someone who is alone can make a positive difference in their life. Even if they say no, you can tell them to come find you if they ever want to join.

These are just a few of the ways you can help friends and peers and have a positive impact on your school and community. If you are a good listener, you might already have friends, family members, or peers coming to you with their problems. The information in this book can help you become an even better listener and give you guidance on what to do if someone shares a more serious problem, such as being depressed or suicidal.

# Formal Helping Roles

Some kids and teens choose to get more training in helping people and become peer counselors, peer mentors, or peer mediators. Read on to learn more about these helping roles.

## PEER COUNSELORS

Peer counseling is when young people help other young people deal with feelings and figure out solutions to problems. It's similar to friends talking to each other. However, peer counselors receive training in basic counseling skills, like listening, reflecting, and offering emotional support, from a school counselor or other professional. But you don't have to be a designated peer counselor to learn these skills and use them to help people you know.

In addition to this one-on-one helping, peer counselors often give presentations to their classmates on a variety of topics, including bullying, eating disorders, internet safety, decision-making, vaping prevention, promoting peace, preventing violence in relationships, substance use, welcoming new students, and reaching out to people who are struggling. They also share what it is like to be a peer counselor to recruit new volunteers.

It's important to remember that peer counselors don't diagnose people. And they can't take the place of professional counselors. However, they are trained to recognize signs of anxiety and depression and can encourage the people they work with to get professional help. They also offer hope that things can get better. As a peer counselor or as a friend, you can share resources for getting professional help. The list on page 122 is a great place to start. You'll also learn more about peer counseling in chapter 2.

## PEER MENTORS

Some young people who seek help from peers have a specific problem they want to solve. They may need to meet only once or twice. Peer counselors can help in these situations. Some other young people need to meet with a peer helper on a consistent basis. This is where peer mentors come in. Unlike peer counselors, who help many classmates with a variety of problems, peer mentors are usually matched with only a few mentees that they follow over a long period of time.

Peer mentors often work with people who have similar problems to what they themselves have been through. Having someone to talk to who has struggled with some of the same issues or situations and can relate helps a person feel understood and may give them hope that things will get better. In some ways, peer mentoring is like being an older sibling.

Peer mentors might help new students adjust to being in middle school or high school, encourage peers looking for friends to get involved in sports or join clubs or other organizations, and help with homework. Some mentors and mentees simply spend time together, engaging in fun activities like playing games or sports.

If you'd like to learn more about becoming a peer mentor, the Alberta Advanced Education Department in Canada offers a *High School Teen Mentoring Activity Book* you can download. See the resources at the end of this book for more.

## PEER MEDIATORS

Another helping role you might take is that of a peer mediator. Peer mediation programs are designed for students to help peers who are having conflict with each other or who have been referred because their behavior got them into trouble. In peer mediation, both sides agree to allow the mediator to help them solve their problem and come up with a solution that everyone can accept. Chapter 7 provides more detailed information on skills you'll need to help others resolve conflict and become an effective peer mediator.

### PEER AMBASSADORS

Planned Parenthood is a not-for-profit organization that provides sexual and reproductive health services and education to people in need, including teens. Various chapters across the United States offer a peer ambassador program. Participants are trained to educate their peers on sexual and reproductive health and rights. They can lead school and community groups in conversations and refer them to care and other resources. You can search for chapters in your area via the national Planned Parenthood website, plannedparenthood.org.

If you'd like to learn more about becoming a peer mediator, the New Jersey State Bar Foundation offers a free guide. See the resources at the end of the book for more.

Referrals for participating in a formal program in one of these roles can come from teachers, school counselors, administrators, or other students. Students can also refer themselves.

In some places, formal programs are set up as diversion programs. For example, if a student is about to be suspended for misbehavior or given a consequence for other problems, they can avoid punishment if they are willing to meet with a peer counselor for a certain number of sessions. Peer mediation can also be an option if the conflict involves another student.

Formal programs might also be proactive, meaning they aim to help young people before problems arise. For instance, if there is a new student in the school and they are sitting alone at lunch, a peer counselor could go up to the student, introduce themselves, and invite the new person to join their friends and meet the group. This proactive helping isn't reserved for peer counselors, mentors, and mediators, however. A simple act of kindness from anyone can go a long way toward reducing bullying and can help in preventing mental health problems in someone who might be socially anxious.

# The Advantages of Helping

Whether you are helping others informally or as a peer counselor, mentor, or mediator, reading this book and gaining helping skills will serve you as well. Growing your interpersonal and communication skills can help you get along better with the people in your life. And these skills will give you ways to reduce interpersonal conflicts, since problems between people often happen when they don't know how to communicate effectively and respectfully.

## PEER COUNSELOR TIP
### Setting Up a Helping Program in Your School

If your school does not have a peer counseling, peer mediation, or peer mentoring program, you might be able to get school officials to start one. Talk with your school counselor, school social worker, or principal about the possibility of setting one up. You can also print out the leader's guide for this book at freespirit.com/leader and share it with them.

Learning helping skills can also help you understand yourself better and develop healthy coping strategies. Understanding yourself and coping well makes it easier to handle your own problems as well as help others with theirs.

By supporting others, you are giving back to your school and wider community, whether your helping role is formal or informal. You can make a big difference in a person's life by listening to them, validating them, believing in them, understanding them, and supporting them through difficult times. Schools and communities become safer places when young people have the skills to help each other and resolve conflicts peacefully.

This kind of helping also sets a good example for your peers and develops your leadership skills. If other kids see you befriending someone who is lonely or standing up for a peer who is being teased or bullied, they might be more willing to do the same. You might inspire them to also make a positive difference and give back to their communities.

If your helping role includes preparing and giving presentations, you are learning skills to help you in future careers, such as sales or teaching. Formal helping roles are also excellent activities to put on college applications.

## PEER COUNSELOR TIP

### Peer Counseling and Careers in Mental Health

Being trained to become a peer counselor can give you an idea of what it might be like to become a professional counselor as a future career. Mental health counselors can have a variety of different backgrounds. Clinical or counseling psychologists have master's or doctoral degrees in psychology, while social workers usually have master's degrees in social work. Licensed professional counselors have master's degrees in counseling. Psychiatrists and psychiatric nurse practitioners can prescribe medication for problems such as ADHD, anxiety, and depression.

Becoming a licensed mental health professional takes many years of education and a lot of hard work. Not everyone can afford the cost of going to college and paying back student loans. It can also be hard to get licensed as a therapist after you finish school because you need a licensed professional to supervise you over a period of a year or more. Finally, you have to pass a licensing exam to be able to practice counseling on your own. Still, being a professional counselor can be very rewarding. Not everyone can say that they have had a role in making other people's lives better.

# Where You Can Help

Where you can help depends on whether you're participating in a formal program or helping in an informal way. Most formal peer counseling, mentorship, and mediation programs are based in middle and high schools. Some high schools even offer them as an elective class for credit. Other formal programs are based in the community. Mental health hotlines are an example of that.

If you're not in a formal helping role, you'll likely use the skills in this book in a variety of settings. Day camps, youth groups, religious programs, scouting programs, and team sports are places where you might support and connect with other young people, in addition to school and home. You might also help people through online activities, like gaming or social media.

# Anti-Bullying Efforts

Some young people choose to help by getting involved in planning anti-bullying initiatives at their school. They may decorate the hallways with positive slogans and hand out cards with emergency contacts, such as suicide or mental health hotlines. They might help with educating peers about bullying, reaching out to new students, passing out information about preventing and standing up to bullying, and checking in with vulnerable peers.

For more information on anti-bullying efforts, check out the resources on the Stop Bullying website (stopbullying.gov). The website also has a Youth Engagement Toolkit that you can download. You'll learn more about how to help people who are being bullied and when to involve adults in chapter 8.

# Which Helping Role Will You Take?

Now that you know some of the helping roles you might take and how they work, think about how you are most interested in helping. This will aid you in figuring out how you want to use this book.

If you want to be a better listener and friend, learning basic helping and problem-solving skills may be enough for you. You can also share the resources in this book with your friends and encourage them to talk to adults if their problems are serious. Chapters 3–6 will be the most important ones for you to read.

If you want to become a trained peer counselor and work with people you may not know, most of this book will be helpful to you. See if your school offers a peer counseling program and if it doesn't, suggest that it develop one.

Peer mentoring is something you can do formally—or informally, if you know kids in your school, neighborhood, or family who might benefit from your help. Peer mediation is mostly done through formal school-based programs, so check with your school to see if it has such a program.

Whatever role you decide to take, know that helping people has lots of advantages! And the good feeling you get from helping others and knowing that someone benefited because of your willingness to lend a hand can make your life more meaningful.

## CHAPTER 2

# Peer Counseling

**Fatima:** "Hey, Jake! Thanks for stopping by our peer counseling open office hours. How's it going? I noticed you seem kind of quiet. Is everything okay?"

**Jake:** "Hi, Fatima. Yeah, well, kind of. Things haven't been going so well at home lately."

**Fatima:** "I'm sorry to hear that. Do you want to talk about it? Maybe there's some way I can help, or at least I can listen."

**Jake:** "I appreciate that. It's not easy to talk about. Are you sure you want to listen?"

**Fatima:** "Yeah, I do. So, tell me what's going on."

# Peer Counseling Defined

If you've decided to become a peer counselor, congratulations! Peer counseling is just as it sounds. It is peers (people your age) counseling or helping each other with problems in their lives. Peer counselors receive training from adult helpers in how to listen to someone's problems and work with them to figure out what to do. In a lot of ways, being a peer counselor is like being a good friend. However, a peer counselor is also different from a friend. With a friend, you might offer advice, telling your friend what you think they should do to handle a problem or sharing how you've handled a similar problem. In peer counseling, your goal is to help the person you are working with come up with their own solutions. You do this by keeping the focus on them, being a sounding board, and asking questions to help them clarify their feelings about the issue and think about possible solutions or steps to take.

Peer counselor programs have been around for many years. Clovis West High School, near Fresno, California, has had one since the 1980s. And at Garey High School in Pomona, California, almost a third of students have taken advantage of their peer counseling program.

Being a peer counselor is, in some ways, like being a professional counselor. Many of the skills you learn, such as reflective listening, using eye contact, and restating or summarizing what people tell you, are all skills that licensed counselors learn in their training. But it's not the same as being a professional. Your ability to help will be limited.

Even if you are not planning on becoming a trained peer counselor, learning these skills can help you become a better friend, family member, and all-around person. If you prefer to take this route, you may choose to skip ahead to chapter 3. But first read the sections The Importance of Giving Hope (page 22) and Keeping Someone's Confidences (page 23) in this chapter, as they provide important information for anyone who wants to offer support and help people with their problems.

# How Peer Counselors Help

If you become a peer counselor, one of the main ways you'll help is by listening to and talking with people about their thoughts, feelings, and problems. You'll also need to show the people you're helping, using reflective listening and summarizing (see pages 51 and 54, respectively), that you are paying attention and that you understand and empathize with them. This can lower your peer's anxiety and make them feel more comfortable talking with you. Talking to someone and hearing their thoughts and feelings repeated by that person can also give your peer insight into steps they might take to solve their problem. Peer counselor training will teach you about the kinds of questions to ask and ways to help people figure out solutions to their problems without coming off as judgmental or critical.

You might also offer suggestions on possible solutions, but only if asked. Be very careful when doing this and always leave the choice up to the person to avoid giving a solution that backfires and makes things worse. If you tell someone to break up with an abusive partner, for example, it could lead to more abuse. If you tell someone to stand up to their parents, they might get punished and blame you for it. You are much better off helping the person think about possible ways to deal with a situation and exploring the pros and cons of each. You could ask,

"What might happen if you decide to talk with your parents about this? What's the best thing that could happen? What's the worst thing?"

As a peer counselor, you can also teach specific skills. Teaching people how to be assertive, how to solve problems, how to resolve conflict, ways to handle bullying, ways to relax, or how to set and work toward goals can be very helpful. You'll likely learn a few skills yourself along the way!

As part of your peer counselor training, you'll learn when someone's problems are beyond your ability to help and how to refer someone to a professional counselor. This is a particularly important part of being a peer counselor. Whether you are a peer counselor or an informal helper, know that you are never expected to give expert advice if someone tells you that they are thinking about suicide, engaging in self-harm, having thoughts about hurting or killing someone, or using drugs or alcohol in a way that is dangerous. Relying on adults in these moments is critical for ensuring people get professional help with serious issues. See chapter 8 for more information about when to seek adult help.

# The Importance of Giving Hope

A very important role of a peer counselor, or of any young person who helps other young people, is to provide hope that things can get better. When people have problems or are experiencing difficult circumstances, they may think that no one can understand them and help them. People who feel hopeless (thinking that things will never get better) or helpless (thinking that they can't do anything to make things better) are at greater risk for depression and suicide. This is why it is so important to share that things can get better and that you will do everything in your power to help with that. Here's one way to do this:

"I'm really glad you shared this with me. I know it's hard to admit when you have a problem, but I know we can figure out some ways to make this situation better for you."

You can also provide hope by helping people build motivation to make the changes they want to make or solve the problems they want to solve. You might do this by pointing out the positive traits you see in the person and expressing your confidence in them:

"From what you've told me, it sounds like when you put your mind to something, you're pretty awesome at getting things done. So if you can use that ability to figure out how to handle this problem, I know you will succeed. You've got this!"

# Keeping Someone's Confidences

Any time you help someone or listen to them talk about emotions and problems, it is essential that you respect their privacy. If you're a peer counselor, you'll know this as *confidentiality*. Promising to keep what people tell you private gives them space and courage to talk to you honestly. So it is never okay to share the things you hear with friends or classmates, or online. Sharing information given to you in confidence is one of the worst things you can do when trying to help someone and will likely erode that confidence. It could make them afraid to open up to anyone else about their problem and might even make the problem worse.

If a person you're helping tells you something that you need to share with an adult, it is best to ask their permission first. Some things, such as vaping or smoking, sneaking out of the house, or skipping school, may be risky but not need immediate attention. But if it is a safety issue, such as abuse or suicidal or homicidal thoughts, you need to talk with a trusted adult right away, before the person leaves the counseling office, given the higher likelihood of harm. Even if they don't want you to share with an adult, safety comes first. You can always offer to share this information together to support them and make it a little easier. See chapter 8 for more information on when and how to reach out to adults. If you are part of a peer counseling program, be sure to ask your adult supervisors on how to handle these kinds of situations before you start working with peers.

# Organizing Support Groups and Clubs

Some students have set up mental health clubs or support groups for kids at their school. These groups are kind of like group peer counseling—everyone has a chance to talk about what's on their mind.

Brooklyn Williams, a teenager at Baldwin High School in Pittsburgh, Pennsylvania, struggled with depression after her mom died. She helped establish the Chill Club at her school to provide a safe space for other teens to talk about mental health. To do so, she received help from The Chill Project, a program that uses mindfulness-based exercises to help students and educators relax and handle stress in positive ways.

Talk with a school counselor, a school social worker, or your school principal if you'd like to try to set up a support group or club at your school.

## BRING CHANGE TO MIND

Bring Change to Mind (BC2M) is a student-led club that's in many high schools in the United States. Teen advisors lead the clubs and introduce mental-health-focused activities to help peers open up and have honest conversations. According to the BC2M website, at the start of the 2022–2023 school year, 450 schools were participating in the program. In one activity, called "Little Worries," club members anonymously write something that's been bothering them that week on a sticky note and post it on a wall in the school. This lets everyone in the school know that they're not the only one who is suffering.

BC2M provides resources for students interested in setting up a group at their school. These include an annual $500 grant for group activities, educational and promotional materials, and access to a club portal containing event and activity information, educational presentations, and a club guidebook. BC2M also holds an annual high school student summit where all club members can meet to learn from leaders in the mental health field and share their experiences. And they provide a free subscription to the Headspace meditation app. For more information on BC2M, check out their website, bringchange2mind.org.

# Advertising Your Program

Students usually refer themselves to peer counseling by contacting an adult in charge of the program. Some schools have open office hours for peer counseling, often during lunch periods. Peer counselors volunteer to be present during these times, and students can walk in to get help. In some schools, peer counselors share contact information (such as a cell number or social media username) so that students can contact them at any time. If you're participating in a peer counseling program at your school, you will likely have guidelines for how students are referred to the program and how they can contact peer counselors.

You might decide to advertise your peer counseling program too. Peer counselors could go from classroom to classroom, giving a short presentation on what they do. Posters, flyers, morning announcements, and school newsletters or newspapers are other great ways to let people know about your peer counseling program, and your school website can be another good place to advertise. You might also advertise on social media.

# What Peer Counseling Is Not

It is important to remember that peer counseling is *not* the same as professional counseling, and that you are never a replacement for a professional therapist or counselor. You can try your best to help people come up with solutions to deal with problems, talk with them about their feelings, offer limited advice, teach some skills, and offer hope that things can get better. But you are not expected to fix their problems or figure out if they're suffering from anxiety or depression. You cannot diagnose these or other mental health problems.

You won't have all the answers, but you will have adults to lean on. You can reach out to parents and other family adults, trusted teachers or coaches, a school counselor, a religious leader, or even your own therapist if you have one. As a peer counselor, you'll also have an advisor who makes sure you are being helpful and not hurtful in your role and who can step in when serious issues arise.

## CHAPTER 3

# Considerations Before Helping

Marco wants to learn more about helping friends and classmates. He's interested in signing up to become a peer counselor. However, he's not sure he's the right person for the job. He tends to get upset easily, and he can be critical over small things. He's actually lost a couple friends as a result. He knows that he can be judgmental at times. Still, he would like to be helpful and thinks he can overcome these obstacles. It might even make him a better person.

Devi, on the other hand, has a lot of friends and acquaintances at school. She is warm and friendly and often volunteers to help others when they need it. People say she is easy to talk to and doesn't judge. She, too, wants to learn more about helping friends and classmates.

Being a good peer counselor or a supportive friend and classmate isn't an easy task. Helping people with their problems can feel like a lot of pressure. Not knowing what to say or do, or being afraid that you'll say or do the wrong thing, can be stressful. In this chapter, you'll learn about the qualities a good helper has. You'll also learn about the ethics of helping and the importance of taking care of yourself.

As you read this chapter, try to be honest with yourself. Are you up to this task? What skills or qualities do you already have that make you a good helper? What ones do you need to gain or improve? Whatever your goals are in reading this book, developing the qualities described next can help you become a better and more supportive friend and classmate and increase your chances of being helpful to the people you care about.

## What Qualities Do You Have?

Imagine yourself sitting down with someone to share something personal. Think about the qualities this person would need to have for you to feel comfortable enough to open up. Or think about a friend or adult you trust and go to when you're feeling upset or need help with a problem. What it is about this person that makes you go to them? Your answer might include some or all of the following qualities:

- **empathetic**—able to understand the thoughts and feelings of others
- **attentive**—able to focus on the person you are helping without getting distracted
- **nonjudgmental**—not quick to judge or criticize someone, even if they have different opinions or attitudes than you
- **open-minded**—willing to work with a variety of people, even if they hold opinions or beliefs different from your own
- **patient**—giving someone the time they need to open up to you and come up with solutions, even if it takes a while
- **kind**—being conscious of your tone of voice to make sure you express care and warmth and choosing your words carefully when talking to people so you don't come across as critical
- **positive**—finding things to like or admire in another person and being willing to share those things with them
- **good listener**—this is more than being caring or empathetic; rather, it involves listening carefully enough to what the other person says to be able to repeat it back in your own words
- **respectful**—not putting someone down for their actions, beliefs, thoughts, or feelings, even if you don't understand them or agree with them; it also means not acting as if you are better than someone else
- **flexible**—going with the flow and being willing to shift your approach when needed
- **humble**—admitting when you are wrong and apologizing when you mess up or say the wrong thing

This may sound like a lot, but these qualities help you be a good friend and person, as well as a good peer counselor. This is why learning to be a better helper can improve your relationships too.

Now comes the hard part. Take an honest look at yourself. You might think about your answers to the following questions or write them in a journal.

- Which of these qualities do you think you have?
- Are there qualities that you lack right now but would be willing to develop?
- Which qualities are the easiest for you? Which are more challenging?
- If you were to ask family, friends, or other close people to rate you on these qualities, what do you think they would say? If you're not sure, are you willing to ask them?

It can feel uncomfortable and scary to look closely at yourself and ask others for their opinions about you. Think of it as an opportunity to grow as a person.

## PEER COUNSELOR TIP

### Peer Counseling Quiz

If you're interested in becoming a peer counselor, the following short quiz can show you how ready you might be. Rate each statement as Always, Often, Sometimes, or Rarely.

- I am good at understanding people's thoughts and feelings.
- I am patient when listening to people.
- I am a good listener and can repeat what others say in my own words.

- I am good at keeping things people tell me private.

- I am respectful when talking to people.

- I am good at not judging people.

- I am accepting of people regardless of their race, ethnicity, family structure, background, sexual orientation, gender identity, religion, culture, or political beliefs.

If you rated yourself as Often or Always on most of these statements, chances are that you're ready to become a peer counselor, mentor, or mediator. If you rated yourself as Sometimes or Rarely on most of these, a helping role may not be right for you quite yet. You can work on developing these skills and qualities, so don't give up!

# Can You Deal with Risky Situations?

In the course of helping people with problems and talking about thoughts and feelings, risky situations—situations where someone's safety is a concern—might come up. Never keep this information to yourself, even if a friend says they're handling it or asks you to keep it a secret. Risky situations are outside of your ability to help, and you need to ask an adult to step in to make sure everyone is safe.

One big risky situation is if someone tells you that they are thinking of killing themselves or someone else. This is *not* something you can handle alone. Talk to a trusted adult immediately. This can ensure that the person stays safe or that they don't hurt anyone else.

Drug and alcohol use are also risky situations. Someone might share that they drink alcohol at parties, smoke weed, or pop pills they find in their medicine cabinet at home. It can be hard to tell how risky someone's use is. Vaping nicotine or having a couple beers with friends on the weekends is different than drinking a whole bottle of liquor or using harder drugs. Driving when drunk or buzzed could result in someone dying. Fentanyl use is dangerous since even tiny amounts can be enough to kill a person. If a person reveals actions or use that put them or other people in danger, seek help from an adult right away.

Physical, sexual, and emotional abuse are also risky situations. If someone tells you they are being abused by an adult or another young person (even if the person is a romantic partner), encourage them to tell a trusted adult. Often, people are afraid to tell an adult in these situations. They may worry about what might happen as a result. You can offer to go with them or help them make the call. If you need to report abuse, telling a licensed therapist or a school counselor or other school adult is a good idea. These people are "mandated reporters." This means that they are legally required to share certain kinds of abuse with the proper authorities, usually child protective service workers or the local police. Pediatricians,

## REPORTING RISKY SITUATIONS

There are a number of people you can talk to if you need to report a risky situation, including:

- teachers, a principal, or other trusted adults at school

- a school counselor, school psychologist, or school social worker

- a parent (yours or someone else's parent whom you trust)

- a doctor or nurse

If it is an emergency and you are not able to find an adult immediately, call 911.

nurses, and law enforcement officers are also mandated reporters. Any report of abuse is something you need to share with a trusted adult who can advise you on how to handle it and step in to make sure everyone is safe. If you're thinking about becoming a peer counselor, ask yourself these questions: Are you able and willing to report risky situations and behaviors? Can you handle revelations like these without freaking out?

It may seem difficult to manage and deal with risky situations. There often aren't clear boundaries for when a person's behavior becomes risky, and the person may not want you to tell anyone else about their situation. Professional therapists and counselors also struggle with this. If you report someone's situation or behavior without their permission, they may not trust you again to share important details. But if you don't tell, something tragic could happen. That's why it's best to report anything that causes you concern for the person's safety or someone else's safety. You'll learn more about how to handle risky situations in chapter 8.

# Do You Like to Talk About Yourself?

Some people like talking about themselves. When others start sharing information, they can relate to it and want to share something similar that happened to them. In a counseling setting, this is known as self-disclosure. You might think that sharing your own problems or the solutions you came up with is helpful. But it can actually be just the opposite. As soon as you share information about yourself, the conversation is in danger of becoming more about you than the person you are trying to help. It can stop them from telling you anything else if they feel you are making everything about you. Professional therapists and counselors struggle with this too. So if you tend to talk about yourself a lot, you'll need to keep that in check when helping someone else!

At the same time, relating to a person's problems can help them feel understood and, if done right, can encourage them to share more. One trick is to keep your personal sharing brief and then quickly turn the conversation back to the other person. Here are some examples:

> "That's the worst! You were all ready to go to the party and your parents changed their mind. That's happened to me before. How did you feel?"

> "Finding out that someone you like just wants to be friends really hurts at first. I've been there too. How do you think you'll handle it?"

Self-disclosure can be helpful, but it is only one of the tools in your helping toolbox. You'll learn more about using self-disclosure and other strategies in chapter 4. If you have a hard time keeping your talking about yourself in check, you may need to work on this before becoming a peer counselor.

# Are You Good at Keeping Secrets?

An especially important part of being a good peer counselor or a good friend is keeping things you are told private—and that means private from everyone. Your best friend, your sibling, and your romantic partner aren't exceptions. People you are helping expect you to keep what they tell you to yourself and not gossip or blab it to everyone. Some people are better at this than others. So be honest with yourself: Are you good at keeping what your friends tell you private, or do you like to gossip and share secrets? Sharing secrets without permission can be hurtful and lead to the end of a friendship or cause the person not to trust you enough to share anything else. The exception to this is when you need to tell an adult about a risky situation to keep people safe. If you're not so good at keeping things private, being a peer counselor may not be for you.

## PEER COUNSELOR TIP
### Ethics of Peer Counselors

Peer counselors, mentors, and mediators must strive to act in ways that are consistent with ethical principles, as should anyone who is helping people with their problems and talking with them about thoughts and feelings. Think of this as a "code of conduct"—guidelines that help you behave in ways that are helpful, rather than hurtful. Professional counselors also have their own code of ethics that they promise to follow in their work.

The National Association of Peer Program Professionals offers a good example of a code of ethics for peer counselors. It includes guidelines around:

- recognizing that the people they help have a right to decide for themselves how they will act

- agreeing to seek support and supervision from adult supervisors

- developing a nurturing personality by being a positive role model for others

- keeping their work with people private and confidential, sharing only with adult supervisors

- reaching out to adult supervisors when any questions of safety, severe family problems, or abuse come up

- promising to reach out for support when feeling overwhelmed emotionally or threatened physically

You don't need to be a peer counselor to follow these ethical standards. Being nurturing, respecting other people's right to make their own decisions, and keeping people's confidences are all good qualities for being a supportive and helpful friend.

# Taking Care of Yourself

While most of the problems people will come to you with won't be as severe as what a professional counselor or therapist may deal with, they can still be stressful. Helping people with their problems is also very rewarding, especially when you see them benefitting from your help! But it can become emotionally draining at times. This is called compassion fatigue or burnout, and it happens when you are working *too* hard to help others without taking care of yourself. If you're burnt out, you may find that you have trouble sleeping, feel tired all the time, or stop caring about the people you're trying to help. For this reason, taking care of yourself emotionally and physically is another important skill to learn.

Be sure you are getting enough sleep. Most young people need at least eight hours. Also try to eat a nutritious and balanced diet. This helps your body and brain function at their best. Getting enough exercise is an excellent stress-reliever that, as an added bonus, helps with sleep.

Mindfulness, or purposefully paying attention to the present moment without judgment, is another popular coping skill for dealing with stress and maintaining a positive outlook. You can read more about it at the Mindfulness for Teens website (mindfulnessforteens.com).

To take care of yourself, it's also important to take time to relax and unwind doing things you enjoy, like listening to or playing music, chatting with friends, doing a craft, playing video games, shooting hoops, reading or writing, or drawing or painting. Be sure to avoid unhealthy ways of dealing with stress, such as using alcohol or drugs, spending too much time online, or avoiding your other responsibilities at home and at school.

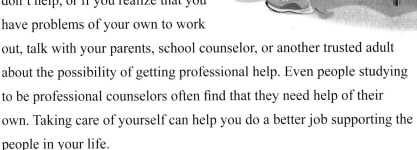

If you're feeling stressed, talk with a peer supervisor or another trusted adult about it. They can help you come up with positive coping strategies to try. If the strategies don't help, or if you realize that you have problems of your own to work out, talk with your parents, school counselor, or another trusted adult about the possibility of getting professional help. Even people studying to be professional counselors often find that they need help of their own. Taking care of yourself can help you do a better job supporting the people in your life.

# Are You Ready?

Reflect on the qualities a good helper has and the other considerations you read about in this chapter. If you think you can handle helping people in a more formal way, and if there is already a peer counseling program in your school, you might decide to participate. Or maybe you'd rather help friends, family, and other people you know. You might start by helping friends and family, and then if that goes well and people respond positively to you, you might decide you want to become a peer counselor later. If you're interested in becoming a peer counselor but your school doesn't have a program, talk to your school counselor or principal to see if they might be willing to start one.

## CHAPTER 4

# Basic Helping Skills

**Nevaeh:** "So, let me see if I have this right. You and your parents had a big fight last night over being on your phone too late. And you feel frustrated because every time you try to talk to them about it, it feels like they lecture you and won't listen to your side of it. Is that it?"

**Milan:** "Yeah! And it happens all the time—whenever I try to tell them how I feel about it, they accuse me of being disrespectful."

**Nevaeh:** "That's the worst! Does that happen all the time, or are there times when they do listen to you?"

**Milan:** "Well, they listen to me better when I'm not already angry. But it's hard to control myself when I'm angry!"

**Nevaeh:** "That's a pretty common problem. Would you like some suggestions on how to do that?"

Learning to help people with their problems takes time. It may seem overwhelming at first—that's understandable! But the more you practice, the easier it becomes. In this chapter, you'll learn basic helping skills so you can show you are paying attention and guide a person to figure out what might be causing their problems.

# Three Tasks for Helping

There are three basic tasks you'll need to remember when helping others: Exploration, Insight, and Action. Peer counselors know them as "stages" in helping, and they provide a good guide whether you are helping in a formal or informal way.

## EXPLORATION

When helping someone, the best place to start is with Exploration. Exploration is when you explore with the person what the problem is. By asking questions, you help them express their thoughts and feelings about the issue so that they can see their problem more clearly. Think of

Exploration as "getting to know" the person and their problem so that you can understand the issue from their point of view. In Exploration, it is important to listen to *how* a person explains their problem and help them express their thoughts and feelings about it. Talking out loud about thoughts and feelings can often lead a person to see them more clearly. By listening and guiding, you are being a "sounding board."

In addition to listening and guiding, be sure to validate the person's thoughts and feelings. When you validate someone's feelings, it shows them that you understand and encourages them to explore their problem more. In this way, Exploration helps you understand a person's issue or problem better before you jump into trying to solve it.

In the example between Nevaeh and Milan, Nevaeh listened to and reflected Milan's feelings. For Milan, this helped them think about how their response to their parents is being perceived as disrespectful. This also sets the stage for the pair to focus on how Milan talks to their parents.

## INSIGHT

The next task is Insight. During Insight, you help the person gain a better understanding of their problem. This is when you ask questions to help them go a bit deeper into the problem—to see if they can figure out why it exists in the first place. Insight may involve helping the person understand their role in creating the problem or making it worse.

Nevaeh might help Milan figure out that how they approach their parents is contributing to their parents' negative reaction. Someone who is having an issue in a romantic relationship might figure out that their partner is really stressed over finals and that is why they are so irritable and lose their cool.

## ACTION

The third and final task is Action. In Action, you help the person figure out what actions they will take to deal with their problem. This is when you ask them about possible solutions. You might ask about what they have already tried, what worked and what didn't, and what they would be willing to try to resolve the problem. This part could also involve setting a goal and listing steps they will take to achieve it. You'll learn more about problem-solving and goal setting in chapter 5.

Milan might decide that they will take a calmer approach when talking to their parents, using deep breathing and remembering that their parents have feelings too.

Depending on the natural flow of your conversation, these tasks might be distinct steps, or they may overlap. You might be asking questions about a person's thoughts and feelings and, while they're answering, they figure out something about the problem they didn't realize before and start talking about solutions. That is perfectly fine! Or they might ask for a suggestion and you have one they can try. The goal is to solve the problem, not to follow a specific path to get there. Still, it can help to think about the three tasks while you are talking with someone. They can also help you move forward if the conversation lags or gets stuck.

Now that you know about Exploration, Insight, and Action, the rest of this chapter shares some basic helping skills you can use during these tasks. You will find these skills useful whether you are helping a friend or family member or helping in your role as a peer counselor.

# PEER COUNSELOR TIP

## Starting a Session

As a peer counselor, most of your helping sessions will start with introductions. You'll welcome your helpee to the session, introduce yourself, explain your role, and ask if they have any questions. Here's an example:

> "Hi! I'm Aidan! Welcome to the peer counseling office! What's your name?" [helpee answers]

> "Nice to meet you! So, I'm a trained peer counselor. I'm here to listen to you, help you figure out what is bothering you, and help you come up with solutions. Of course, I'm not a professional counselor, but I can help you get a therapist if you like. What we talk about during our session is private. I'm not allowed to tell anyone else about you or your problems. I do have an adult supervisor who can help me in helping you better. If you tell me about risky behaviors where you or someone else is being hurt or is in danger of being hurt, I am required to talk with my supervisor about it to make sure you are safe. Do you have any questions before we start?"

Before you can start helping someone, it is important to establish a rapport with them. This means that you are comfortable talking with each other. It makes it easier for the person to open up to you. To build rapport, you might start out by asking a few questions to get to know the person before going into their problem. Some good questions are what grade they're in, how they like school, what they like to do for fun, if they have any pets, and if they are involved in any sports or other activities.

After the introduction and get-to-know-you questions, you can ask why the person is seeking help. Keep it simple though. You might try one of these options:

- "What brings you here today?"
- "How can I help you today?"
- "So, what's going on?"
- "What did you want to talk about?"

# Attending Skills—Showing You're Listening

Attending is a basic helping skill. It means paying full attention to the person you are helping and communicating that attention to the person so they know you're listening. Here are some of the attending skills good helpers have.

**Eye contact.** Looking at someone while you are listening to them conveys interest and caring. If you have trouble with eye contact, try looking at just one of the person's eyes. Do your best to make eye contact when you are talking as well. Don't stare, though! That makes people uncomfortable. If you find your attention wandering, bring your eyes back to the person. Pay attention to the person's body language too. If they seem uncomfortable with your eye contact, it is okay to look away more often or look down, perhaps with your hand on your chin, to show that you are thinking about what they are telling you.

**Body language.** Pay attention to your body language. Facing the person shows your interest and that you are open to what they have to say. Nodding your head as they are talking also shows that you are paying attention and that you get it. Be sure to watch your facial expressions and try to keep your face neutral, encouraging, and open. Reacting too much to something a person says, such as raising your eyebrows, can come across as judgmental. If you have a tendency to look angry or annoyed even when you don't feel that way, you'll want to work on this!

**Affirming.** Affirming means making positive statements about the person or what they're saying to encourage them and make it easier for them to share more. Here are some examples: "Wow—that was really brave of you!" "How did you get yourself to tell her, knowing she'd be upset?" "You really want to avoid hurting their feelings—that's very caring of you." Saying something as simple as *yeah*, *I know*, *wow*, or *mmhmm* can also be affirming—it lets the person know you're with them and paying attention.

**Reflecting.** Also called summarizing, this is when you reflect back to the person what you heard them say, using your own words and some of theirs. It also includes checking with the person to make sure you understood them correctly. Here are a couple examples: "What I am hearing from you is that you are upset about an argument you had with your best friend and are unsure how to go about handling it so you don't lose your friendship. Is that right?" "It really bothers you when your parents tell you to do something just as you were about to do it. It sounds like this happens a lot." Summarizing can also be used at the end of a helping session in a broader way. You'll read more about that later.

**Noticing.** Noticing is another important attending skill. This is when you pay close attention to how the other person reacts to what they are talking about or how they respond to what you are asking or saying. You might notice as someone is talking that they start frowning, or looking away, or shifting in their chair. Essentially, you are reading their body language and using it to try to figure out what they are thinking or feeling. For example, if a person stiffens up or shifts in their chair after something you said, you might guess that they are feeling uncomfortable. Raising their eyebrows may mean they are surprised at what you said.

USE THE ACRONYM **ENCOURAGES** TO REMEMBER THESE ATTENDING SKILLS.

**E** = Maintain **eye contact**, but don't stare (and don't look away too often).

**N** = Nod as a way of showing you are listening.

**C** = **Cultural differences** matter—be aware and respectful of how your actions might be perceived. For example, in some cultures, direct eye contact is considered rude.

**O** = Keep an **open stance**—sit facing the person, don't fold your arms, and try to lean forward a bit.

**U** = **Use acknowledgments** such as *mmhmm, yeah,* and *right*.

**R** = Relax and be yourself.

**A** = Avoid **distracting behaviors**, such as fidgeting, checking your phone, or fiddling with your hair.

**G** = Try to use the same **grammatical style** or language as the person you're talking with (this can be hard to do without proper training, so don't worry about it too much). If you're talking to someone much younger than you, for example, try to use easier words or words you hear them say. However, this doesn't mean you should mimic how they talk, which would be rude.

**E** = Listen with a "third **ear**" to what the person is saying (and perhaps not saying) and how they are behaving with you. You can do this by paying attention to a person's body language and how they react when you're talking with them or asking questions.

**S** = Think about **space**; don't sit too close to the person or too far away.

(Hill 2020)

**Silence.** It may surprise you, but silence is an important attending skill. Many people are uncomfortable with silence and are too quick to fill the space with talking. But silence can be a respectful way of giving someone more time to process how they're feeling and figure out what they want to say. If the person you're talking with seems uncomfortable with silence, or if you have waited more than twenty seconds, you can break it by asking a follow-up question.

# Asking Questions—Getting More Info

Whenever you're helping someone, it is a good idea to ask questions to find out how the person is feeling and what goals they have for themselves. There are three types of questions you can use: open questions, closed questions, and clarifying questions. All three can be helpful, though some more than others.

**Closed questions** are those that can be answered with a simple *yes* or *no* or with a specific answer. For example:

- "How long has this problem bothered you?"
- "Did you tell them how you felt about it?"
- "How often do you get into fights?"
- "Are you feeling sad today?"
- "What did they say next?"
- "Have you had this problem before?"

While these kinds of questions can be helpful, they often close down communication if you ask too many of them. By asking closed questions, you are doing most of the talking and the person you are helping isn't encouraged to share more with you after they answer the question. The conversation just stops, and you have to think of another question to ask.

If you ask a lot of these questions in a row, the person might feel as if they're being interrogated.

**Open questions** tend to be more helpful than closed questions because they require more than a simple answer. For example, "How would you like your relationship with your parents to be?" (open) invites a more detailed response than, "Do you want to get along better with your parents?" (closed). Another benefit of open questions is that they make the person think before they answer. Here are some examples of open questions:

- "Who are some people you could go to for help with this?"
- "What are some ways you might be able to solve this problem?"
- "When does this problem happen?"
- "Why do you think this issue is so hard for you?"
- "How do you usually handle it when this happens?"

**Clarifying questions** are used when you need to get more information. They can get people to think more deeply about their problem and help them in coming up with solutions. Clarifying questions are often helpful after you have summarized what you heard someone say. You might ask:

- "So, you want to bring your grades up, but it seems like nothing works. Can you give me some examples of things you've tried so far?"
- "Sounds like you and your girlfriend are getting into fights and you're not sure if you should stay together. What are some of the things you fight about?"
- "Hmm. Sounds like you were really excited to try out for the school play. Even though you made it, you didn't get the part you wanted. That can be really disappointing. And

showing up at rehearsals just makes you feel sad and now you're thinking of quitting. What might be some reasons you'd want to stay?"

Asking questions, whether closed, open, or clarifying, is helpful in giving you more information about the problem and giving the person you're helping a broader perspective on it. This greater understanding will help when it comes to finding solutions.

# Reflecting—Talking About Feelings

In addition to being an attending skill, reflecting is one of the most common helping tools you'll use. When you reflect, it is important to focus specifically on the person's emotions. This makes it easier for them to identify, clarify, and express what they feel. Usually, people feel better after sharing their feelings about a problem and are more open to taking action to deal with it. Reflecting can also help the person explore the range of emotions they have about a problem or issue. Here's an example:

> **Jessica:** "I can't believe she was talking about me behind my back!"
>
> **Carlos:** "Sounds like you're pretty upset about it."
>
> **Jessica:** "Yeah, definitely. It also hurts. I thought we were friends."
>
> **Carlos:** "You didn't think a friend would do that to you. Maybe you're feeling disappointed as well?"
>
> **Jessica:** "I think so. I thought I could trust her."

As someone talks about what's bothering them, try to listen for any feelings they are sharing. Basic emotions, such as happy, sad, worried, nervous, and mad, are the ones you'll hear the most. Sometimes, you'll have a sense that there is a feeling behind what someone is telling you, even if they didn't use an emotion word. In these situations, you can

## RESPONDING TO BIG FEELINGS

When you're talking with people about big feelings such as sadness, anxiety, or anger, it can be hard to know how to respond. Should you try to cheer them up? Calm them down? Tell them not to worry so much? Responding to big feelings can be a little easier if it's a friend, family member, or someone else you know well. In these cases, a hug might help. But ask first. Not everyone feels comfortable getting hugs, and sometimes people who are upset don't want one.

Usually, it helps to keep your voice low and gentle. If someone is crying, offer them a tissue. Don't talk too much or start offering solutions right away. Just being quiet, maintaining eye contact, and giving the other person a chance to process what they're feeling is all you need to do. You might say:

- "I'm sorry this is so hard."
- "I know it's a lot to handle."
- "I can see how upsetting this is for you."

If the person's big feelings are related to anger, you can use a louder tone (but not yelling) to let them know you understand how angry they are. You might say:

- "That really sucks!"
- "No wonder you're so mad!"
- "I'd be really upset, too, if that happened to me!"

If this doesn't help them calm down, you can try lowering your voice so that they have to lower theirs to hear you. For some people, this helps them calm down.

help the person identify that feeling. Reflecting like this is also a way of checking in to make sure you heard them correctly. For example:

> "From what you're telling me, I'm guessing that it also hurt your feelings a bit when he didn't bother to text you back after he said he would. Is that right?"

Here are some other examples of how you might reflect a person's feelings:

- "So, you're feeling really sad about your friend leaving."
- "You seem pretty upset over this."
- "Sounds like you're a bit nervous about it too."
- "Maybe you're feeling mad as well?"
- "It's been hard for you in dealing with this problem."
- "If I heard you right, it sounds like you have mixed feelings about this. Part of you wants to tell them off and be done with it, but the other part of you still hopes that you can work it out. Is that right?"

To get a sense of how strong a person's feelings are, you can ask them to rate them. Some people find this helpful. For example:

> "On a scale from 1 to 10, with 1 being not at all sad about it and 10 being so sad about it that you can't stand it, how sad would you say you are?"

By rating how strong a feeling is, whether it is sadness, anger, hurt, or another emotion, a person can figure out how big a problem is for them and how important it is to address it. You'll learn more about rating scales in chapter 5.

# Restating—Summarizing What's Been Said

Repeating back what you hear someone saying, using some of their words and some of your own, is known as restatement or summarizing. By summarizing what you heard, usually with fewer words, you show the person that you are listening closely to what they are telling you. Summarizing also helps you make sure you understood them correctly. It is helpful to summarize what the person said before you start talking about solutions.

## PEER COUNSELOR TIP
### Summarizing in a Session

Reflecting or summarizing is an attending skill, but it can also be used in a broader way. If you are a peer counselor, it can be helpful to use summarizing to give a detailed overview of the session. This gives the person a chance to think about their problem in a new way. But you don't want to repeat everything they just told you using the same words. That doesn't work so well. Here's an example:

> "So, Eliot, we've talked about a lot today. We started talking about how stressed you are over your low grades. You want to do better, but it seems that every time one of your grades improves, the others get worse. And it's not just that. Your parents getting on your case just upsets you and makes you not even want to try. Then you're not just stressed, you're also mad at your parents for not understanding how hard you're trying. And a little sad too. Did I get that right?"

# Self-Disclosure—Sharing Your Experiences

Some counselors talk about their own experiences as a way of helping people. This is called self-disclosure. Sharing something about yourself can make the other person feel less alone and more understood. It also lets them know that you can relate to what they're going through. When it works, the other person will usually say something that lets you know you got it right.

It can be tricky, though, as you don't want to make the conversation all about you. That's the danger with self-disclosure. As a result, it's best not to do too much of this, if any. If you think a little self-disclosure might help because you can relate to what the other person is telling you, keep it brief and make sure you pay attention to how they react to your sharing information about yourself. Once you've shared, quickly bring the conversation back to how the person you're talking with is feeling. This keeps the focus on them. Here are a few examples of self-disclosure:

**Jackson:** "It really upsets me when my parents ground me for something that wasn't my fault! I can't stand it!"

**Ava:** "Sounds like that is very frustrating for you. I don't like it when my parents do that either! How often does this happen for you?"

**Amelia:** "I studied so hard for my chemistry test and I still failed it. I feel so stupid."

**Kai:** "That really sucks, especially after trying so hard! I felt pretty bad when I failed my physics test too. Any ideas on what caused you to fail it? Like, was the test different from what you expected?"

If the person seems happy that you shared your situation, you could ask if they'd like to hear how you handled it. If not, maybe you should skip self-disclosure in the future and keep the focus on them.

Self-disclosure is often part of talking with a friend or family member, so it is generally safer and more helpful to use with these people than in a peer counseling session. When you share things about yourself, similar situations you have been in, or feelings that you've had with friends and family, it can deepen your connection with them. Still, take care not to make the conversation all about you. As with peer counseling, be brief and pay attention to the other person's reaction. If they seem happy that you shared, that's great. If it doesn't seem to help, then keep the focus on their thoughts and feelings.

# Unhelpful Reactions

It is best to tread carefully when helping someone or talking with them about their problems, as some actions or statements can be seen as rejecting or hurtful. For example, interrupting someone when they are in the middle of telling you something is basically talking over them. It gives them the impression that you think what you have to say is more important than what they have to say. It's also rude. At the same time, when you're in the middle of a discussion and you feel you're connecting and maybe excited about what you want to add, you might end up interrupting without realizing it. If you do, just apologize. You can say, "Sorry, I interrupted you—go ahead."

Review the following examples of unhelpful comments. See if you can think of a time when you said something similar to a friend or a time when someone said something like that to you. What happened? How did you or your friend feel? This will make it easier to avoid doing the same thing when you're trying to help someone else.

**Unhelpful comment:** "Oh, you think that's bad? You should hear what happened to me!"

**Why it's unhelpful:** This reaction minimizes a person's problems by making them think that you have it worse. It is not a contest. Any time you start talking about yourself, you risk losing the person you are talking to. It's better to say something like, "That sounds awful! How do you feel when that happens?"

**Unhelpful comment:** "You should just break up! You don't have to let anyone treat you that way!"

**Why it's unhelpful:** This is not only advice giving, but can come across as putting the person down, as if the decision to break up should be an easy one. Here's a better response: "It sounds like it upsets you so much when your partner treats you that way that you wonder whether you should stay together or break up. Is that right?"

**Unhelpful comment:** "You're sick and tired of being teased by your brother. He's such a jerk!"

**Why it's unhelpful:** Even if someone is upset with another person, it doesn't mean that they don't care about the person. Putting the other person down or speaking badly of them can make it worse. Here's a better response: "It sounds like it really upsets you when your brother teases you and you wish he would stop."

**Unhelpful comment:** "You shouldn't feel so bad about yourself. You're a great person!"

**Why it's unhelpful:** This might well be true. But if someone says they feel bad about themselves and you tell them they shouldn't, you are basically invalidating their feelings. Here's a better response: "Feeling bad about yourself can be pretty rough. How is that for you?"

Even the best of counselors sometimes makes unhelpful comments. We're all human and we all make mistakes. The important thing is to apologize if you end up hurting someone's feelings. By learning what works and what doesn't work, you will be less likely to make unhelpful comments in the future.

After reading this chapter, you might feel a bit overwhelmed by all the helping skills you'll need to learn. Don't worry. It takes time to learn these skills, but using them will get easier as you work at it, and they will feel natural once you've mastered them. The good news is that you can practice them anytime you talk with someone else. Growing these skills can help you be supportive and helpful to people in your life right now and in the future..

## CHAPTER 5

# Helping People Find Solutions

**Manuel:** "Hey, Osman! Can I talk with you about something important?"

**Osman:** "Sure! What's up?"

**Manuel:** "I just found out that a bunch of my other friends had a sleepover and I wasn't invited."

**Osman:** "Ouch. That sucks."

**Manuel:** "Yeah, it pissed me off too. I've invited a lot of those guys over before and I don't know why they wouldn't invite me."

**Osman:** "Can you think of a reason they wouldn't have invited you?"

**Manuel:** "No, I thought things were good between us."

**Osman:** "What do you plan to do about this?"

**Manuel:** "I don't know. I don't want sound desperate or anything."

**Osman:** "Would you like some suggestions?"

**Manuel:** "Sure!"

Once you've used the skills you learned about in chapter 4 to help a person express their thoughts and feelings and get some insight into their problem, you'll be ready to help them in the third task: Action. The Action task is where you help the person come up with solutions and you share information and resources. You can also teach some skills that will help the person manage their emotions more effectively and make their life easier in the future.

In this chapter, I share ways you can help people take action, including giving information and teaching basic skills such as being assertive, changing thinking, and using relaxation techniques. I also share some unhelpful actions to avoid, and show peer counselors how to end a counseling session. While the goal of this chapter is to teach you skills to help others, you can also use the strategies yourself!

# Building Motivation to Make a Change

The first step in helping people take action is building their motivation to make a change. One way of doing this is to ask the person how motivated they are and how confident they are that they can solve the problem or reach their goal. Depending on what they tell you, you can then help them identify ways to boost their confidence and increase their motivation to find a solution.

## READINESS RULERS

One often-used method by professional counselors is the readiness ruler, also known as a rating scale. The counselor will ask a person to rate how strongly they feel about something, usually on a scale from 1 to 10. Here's an example:

> "On a scale of 1 to 10, where 1 means not important at all and 10 means extremely important, how important is it to you to solve this problem?"

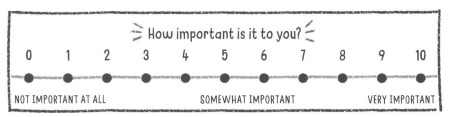

This same scale can be used to measure how confident someone is in their ability to solve a problem.

> "On a scale of 1 to 10, where 1 means not confident at all that you can make a change and 10 means extremely confident, how confident are you that you can solve this problem?"

If a person rates the problem as important to solve and they are confident they can do it, they are well on their way to handling it successfully. If they are less confident, between 1 and 5, you can help them figure out why they feel this way and what they can do to boost their confidence.

You might use a readiness ruler if you're helping someone with a problem around getting better grades, handling anger more effectively, making friends, dealing with friend drama, or getting along with siblings or adults at home. They tend to work well with most types of problems but are especially helpful when the person is unsure if they are ready to work on solving a problem or making a change.

Here are some other questions you can use to help someone figure out how they want to deal with a problem:

- "How much do you want to make this change?"
- "What might make it harder for you to change?"
- "What could help you make this change?"
- "Who might help you make this change?"

# Helping People Find Solutions

**Shalee:** "So it sounds like you've decided to quit the basketball team but you're not sure how to tell your coach and your parents. You're worried that they won't take it well. How do you think you might break it to them?"

**Noah:** "Well, I could tell them that it's not fun anymore and that my grades have dropped. That's not so good if I'm going to get into college."

**Shalee:** "That sounds like a good start! What if they get upset with you? How would you handle that?"

**Noah:** "I'd tell them that I understand that they're upset, but that it's my life and my grades are important to me too. I can't play my best if my heart isn't in it. That's not fair to my teammates."

**Shalee:** "Good point! Sounds like you have a plan. How confident are you that you're ready to do this?"

After you have spent time understanding someone's concerns, the next step is helping them come up with solutions to their problems. It's usually best to help brainstorm possible solutions instead of telling them what you think they should do. Here are some questions to get you started:

- "What are your thoughts about how to solve this problem?"
- "What are some things you have thought of that might help?"
- "How do you think you might want to handle this?"
- "Have you had this problem before? What did you do then to solve it?"
- "Is there anyone in your life who you think might give you some good suggestions?"
- "Have you talked to anyone else about this? What did they tell you? What do you think about that?"

Sometimes, people you are helping will come up with ideas on their own and will feel better about taking action. For some, this may be all the help they need. Others might benefit from more specific suggestions, information on things they can do, or resources they can check out for themselves.

If someone is having trouble coming up with solutions (which may be why they came to you in the first place!), you can offer suggestions. But don't tell them what they *should* or *need to* do. That's never a good idea, and it can backfire if you tell them to do something they aren't comfortable doing or that makes the problem worse. It's better to try to offer your suggestions in a milder way. Refer to the conversations between Osman and Manuel and Shalee and Noah for examples of how to do this. You might also try:

- "Would you like to hear some suggestions on how you might handle this problem?"
- "I have a few ideas of what you might do—is it okay to share them with you?"

Once the person gives you the okay, you can share your suggestions. But share them in a way that leaves it up to the person to decide if and what they'll try.

- "Well, one thing you might try would be _____. How does that sound to you?"
- "Would you consider _____?"
- "What about doing some research on _____?"
- "Maybe you could _____. What do you think?"

Here's an example:

> "Maybe you can schedule a time to sit down with your parents and let them know you want to come up with a better plan for getting chores done. What do you think of this idea?"

Notice in the example that you're not telling the person what to do. The words you use aren't forceful—you're not giving an order. Asking gently makes it clear to the person that it's okay not to take your

suggestions or even listen to them. They might want to think about it
some more on their own before coming up with solutions too.

# Giving Information

It is never your job to solve people's problems for them or come up
with all the answers. However, if someone is talking to you about a
problem and they aren't sure how to handle it, you can offer to give
them some information or resources that might help. Just be sure to ask
permission first.

> **Trevor:** "I can't decide which classes to take next year."
>
> **Asiya:** "Would you be willing to talk to the school
> counselor about that? She may have some good ideas."

> **Sara:** "I'm really having trouble getting up in the morning
> for school. I try to go to bed on time, but it's hard when
> my friends are online or I'm looking at social media. My
> parents are on my case about it and are threatening to take
> my phone at night."
>
> **Micah:** "That's a tough one. I think we all struggle
> with that. Have you considered using the 'do not
> disturb' function on your phone? That works well for
> some people."

Another common way you can give information is to recommend
books that might be helpful. If there's a book you read on handling
anxiety, for example, you might suggest that as a resource. Your school
counselor can give you suggestions. Librarians, at both your school

and your local library, are another good resource. You can also give out helpline phone numbers that people can call if they are having a crisis. Websites, social media sites, and YouTube channels can also be good resources, though be careful with social media and YouTube, as the information you find won't always be accurate. The resources at the end of this book list a number of good mental health resources you can share.

# Teaching Skills

Part of professional counseling is teaching people specific skills that can help them manage their emotions and deal with their problems. While it is best left to professional counselors to teach most skills, there are some that are easy for young people to teach. You will probably have heard of most of them. The following sections share the skills, along with tips for teaching them to friends, family members, and peers. You might also use them yourself!

## ASSERTIVENESS

Assertiveness is one skill that you can teach. Being assertive means standing up for yourself and what you believe and asking for what you want without being aggressive or rude. Many people have trouble being assertive. They may want to please others or might worry about hurting other people's feelings or making them angry. But keeping feelings in isn't always a great idea. And being too passive and not saying what you want or need means that you'll be upset without ever having tried to solve the problem. Remember, other people can't read your mind to know how you are feeling and what you are wanting.

Being assertive also means staying calm. Raising your voice or yelling at someone to stop hurting your feelings usually makes people feel defensive. They might yell back, which just results in both of you being upset. Here's an example of someone who wants to join in a game, and how they share what they want aggressively, passively, and assertively.

Aggressive: "Let me play with you! It's not fair that I can't play!"

Passive: "I wish I could play with you."

Assertive: "I'd like to join your game. Is it okay if I play?"

Some people deal with anger or frustration by being passive-aggressive. This is a way of showing anger indirectly, or passively. A passive-aggressive response might be to say you'll do something someone asks of you but have no intention of following through, or to do it slowly or poorly as a way to punish the other person for asking you. A common example is "forgetting" to do your chores or homework after saying you'll do them. This usually results in bad feelings for both people and doesn't resolve the issue.

Being assertive can help in many situations in life. This is why it's such a great skill to share with others. Assertiveness also builds self-esteem, since assertive people stand up for and stay true to themselves. It's a great skill to lean on when you feel pressured into doing something you don't want to do. And you can use it when saying no to things that are dangerous or that you don't agree with, such as using drugs, stealing, sneaking out of the house, cheating, spreading rumors, being intimate with someone, or bullying.

When communicating how you feel or what you think in an assertive way, it often helps to stand up straight, make eye contact with the other person, and use their name. I-messages are a good way to assertively share what you feel. These statements start with *I* and share your feelings and perspective. Here are some examples:

- "Bruno, I don't want to hang out with you and your friends. I've done it before and I never have a good time. I feel upset when you keep pushing me to do it."
- "Grandma, I get mad when you keep bugging me about my homework. My grades are good. I want you to stop."
- "Mr. Jones, it really embarrasses me when you call on me in class to answer a question and I don't know the answer."

Sharing tips for being assertive with the people you're helping can aid them in a variety of situations. If someone needs more help with this, you can share these assertive ways of saying no. Remind them to stand up straight, look at the person if they're comfortable doing that, and speak calmly and firmly.

- "I'm not comfortable doing that."
- "No. I'm sorry, but I don't want to do that."
- "I don't want to go out with you."
- "Thanks, but no thanks!"
- "No, I don't do drugs."
- "Sorry, but I don't want to skip school."

Let the person know that if anyone keeps pressuring them after they said no, they can just repeat themselves in the same calm tone as many times as they need to. This is called the "broken record" strategy. If you stay calm and firm when you are saying no, people figure out that you're not going to budge.

You can offer to practice being assertive with the person. You can pretend to be the person they want to talk to, and they can practice sharing their feelings in an assertive way. This is called role playing, and it can be a fun way to learn a new skill. You might even ask someone to role-play with you when you need practice being assertive.

## POSITIVE SELF-TALK

Often, people say negative things about themselves that make them feel worse. Their self-talk might sound a bit like this:

- "I'm not good enough."
- "No one likes me."
- "I'll never pass this test."
- "I'll just make it worse."
- "They'll never want to go out with me. I shouldn't even ask."

One strategy that can help break this habit is to replace negative self-talk with positive self-talk. Positive self-talk is like giving yourself a pep talk to boost your confidence. Even if the positive statements don't feel true yet, repeating them to yourself can make a big difference. Athletes and performers often use positive self-talk before a game or performance.

When teaching this skill to someone you're helping, start by asking the person for some positive and helpful things they could say to themselves. If they need ideas, here are some examples you can suggest:

- "I've got this!"
- "I can try my best!"
- "I don't have to be perfect."
- "I won't know if it will work until I try."
- "If I study, I know I can pass this test!"
- "I'm a nice person, and people will want to be my friend."
- "I can handle it even if things don't go my way."

- "I can be a good friend."

Keep in mind that positive self-talk works best if used every day. These positive daily messages are also known as affirmations. The Happier Human website has a list of 67 affirmations you can share with someone you're helping or use yourself to boost self-confidence (happierhuman.com/positive-affirmations-teens). There are also plenty of apps that can help. An internet search will yield many options. You can even suggest that the person look up apps they could try while they are with you.

## THE MIRACLE QUESTION, OR "FAKE IT 'TIL YOU MAKE IT"

This technique is common in therapy, but you can use it too. Ask:

> "If a miracle happened and you woke up with your problem solved, how would you know? What would you be doing differently? Could you act this way now, as if the problem were miraculously solved?"

This "miracle question" can help people realize that they have the power to make a change if they change how they think about their problem. You might also think of this as "fake it 'til you make it." Even if you don't feel confident in yourself, acting as if you do can help you start behaving in ways that a confident person would. It doesn't mean you're ignoring the problem or pretending it doesn't exist. Instead, think of it like playing the role of a confident person in a school play. The longer you or the person you're helping plays the role, the easier it becomes, until it is no longer a role. It becomes part of how you feel about yourself. This also works with self-esteem. If you act as if you feel good about yourself, and people respond positively to that, in time, you'll start believing it yourself.

## JOURNALING

A journal can be a wonderful and safe place to write about thoughts and feelings. And writing thoughts and feelings often gets them out of your head so you can take a closer look at them. For some people, writing in a journal can feel like talking to someone about their problems. Some young people I've worked with have described journaling as having a best friend you can share things with and not worry how they'll react.

Journaling can also work well to help people cope with anger. Writing in a journal as if you're talking to someone you're upset with helps you let some anger out. You might find that you're not so mad afterward. It can also help you stay calmer if you decide you want to talk to the person later.

Talking to a pet is good for this too!

There are no rules about journaling, so it's an easy skill to teach. You can start by encouraging the person you're helping to write about how their day was, what problems they're having, what's going well, what's not going so well, what they learned that day, and how they want to handle a problem. I also have a downloadable page with information about journaling on my website that you can share (cfcc.info/handouts/journalkids.pdf).

Some people use online journals or take notes on their phones, tablets, or other devices. This can help keep a journal private. A simple internet search for "digital journals" will yield a number of free and paid options.

## GRATITUDE JOURNAL

Different from general journaling, a gratitude journal is a place where you keep track of the things you're grateful for every day. Keeping a gratitude journal often helps people feel more positive about their life and the world in general.

You can ask a person you're helping if they would be willing to write down at least three things they are grateful for each day. These can be as small or as big as the person likes. If they're having trouble getting started, you might share a few examples: having a safe house to live in, having a day of gorgeous weather, being smart or athletic or artistic, having good friends or a caring family, or enjoying a delicious meal or tasty snack. If the person doesn't want to write in a journal, they could just say the things they're grateful for to themselves each night. Gratitude helps people focus on the positives in life rather than the negatives, which usually helps them feel better. If you or someone you're helping already has a general journal, gratitude can be easily added to a journaling routine without needing to keep a separate journal.

## UNTWISTING THINKING

When people feel upset about things that happen to them, it's usually not just about the event or situation itself. Negative messages a person tells themselves about an event or situation and the negative thoughts they have about it also come into play. These are commonly called Automatic Negative Thoughts, or ANTs as coined by psychiatrist Dr. Daniel Amen. One way to feel better about yourself and your situation is to get rid of these ANTs and replace them with Positive Energizing Thoughts, or PETs. PETs are a much more helpful way of thinking about things.

You can teach someone to identify their negative thoughts about a problem and talk back to them with something more positive and helpful. Here are a couple examples you can share:

"If you fail a test and tell yourself, 'I failed—I'm so stupid. I'll never get good grades,' you'll feel worse about it and be less likely to try in the future. If instead you tell yourself, 'I'm disappointed in my test grade, but I really didn't study hard so that's why I got a bad grade. If I study harder next time, I know I can do better,' you are more likely to try harder in the future."

"So, you finally got the nerve to ask him out after months of thinking about it and he turned you down. That's really hard. But if you tell yourself that you're not 'dating material' and no one will ever want to date you, you'll likely just give up and be lonely. Instead, if you tell yourself that not every person you ask out is going to be attracted to you and that you just have to keep trying until you find the right person for you, it will be easier to try again."

Changing ANTs to PETs is an example of cognitive behavioral therapy (CBT). The idea behind CBT is that a person's thoughts or beliefs about a problem or situation determine how they feel about it. Consider the following scenarios:

If your mom yells at you for not cleaning your room, you might feel mad and sad, especially if you tell yourself she doesn't care about you or is trying to upset you on purpose. If instead you tell yourself that your mom is upset because she had a hard day and because you didn't keep your promise to clean your room, it might be easier for you to react calmly. And maybe, just maybe, you'll actually clean your room to make her happy.

If you tell yourself that people don't want to be your friend because you're lousy or boring, you might blame yourself for struggling to find friends and might not put yourself out there. If you instead tell yourself that people have different ideas of what they want in a friend and that maybe you don't have a lot in common with a specific person, you might not take it so personally and be more willing to try making different friends.

If you are helping someone, and you notice that they are having ANTs about their problem or themselves, you can help them learn to untwist these negative thoughts. You might ask:

- "Is there a different way you can think about this problem?"
- "Might there be another reason that you failed the test, instead of labeling yourself as dumb?"
- "I notice you keep talking about the worst thing that could happen. What's the best thing that could happen if you take a chance and put yourself out there?"

Thinking negatively is in some ways like a bad habit. People do it automatically, without realizing they're doing it. Feeling sad or depressed often makes negative thoughts worse. It can help to approach untwisting thinking as developing a new, positive habit. You will need to practice it repeatedly until it becomes more automatic, similar to learning to make a basket, catch a ball, land a cartwheel, or speak more clearly. Remind yourself (or the person you're helping) to be patient and give it time. Habits don't change overnight.

## RELAXATION SKILLS

When you or someone you're helping is having a problem, it can add a lot of stress to an already stressful world. Built-up stress makes it harder for people to sleep, focus on school, or get along with others. Learning relaxation skills can help a person calm down and reduce their stress.

One relaxation skill is exercise. Exercise is a great way to relieve stress—even just a few minutes can help—and it is something anyone can do. You can try taking a walk, playing a sport, doing some chair yoga poses, or gentle stretching—anything that gets the body moving.

Another relaxation skill is deep breathing. Breathing in slowly to the count of five and breathing out slowly to the count of five signals to the brain that it should tell the body to calm down. The TeensHealth website (teenshealth.org) has a "Relaxation Exercises: Breathing Basics" video you can share.

Guided mediation is another skill you can use. This involves listening to someone with a soothing voice describe a relaxing scene—often while music plays—to take your mind off your stress. An internet search will yield many such videos and resources.

You can share these relaxation ideas with people you are helping and ask if they'd be willing to try one or more to reduce stress. You can also use them yourself.

Finding solutions to problems and learning some basic skills such as being assertive, learning to relax, and changing how you think about a situation are all valuable strategies to improve quality of life, for yourself and those you are helping. So give these strategies a try in your own life. If they help, you'll have personal experience to draw on when helping others!

# PEER COUNSELOR TIP
## Ending a Session

When you're ready to end a peer counseling session, it helps to summarize what you talked about during the session and what the person plans to do to solve their problem. This gives you a chance to check that you heard what they said correctly. It also helps to get feedback. Here are some examples of how you might summarize a session and ask for feedback:

- "It sounds like you've figured out what you want to say to your friends when they make fun of you. I hope I've been able to help you with that."

- "How do you think our talk went? Was it helpful? Did I say or do anything that didn't feel so good?"

- "You did a great job coming up with some goals for yourself in the next few months."

You can also encourage them to come back and speak with you again if they would like, even if it's just to tell you how things turned out.

## CHAPTER 6

# Teaching Problem-Solving Skills

**Riley:** "I'm trying to figure out what colleges to apply to. I have a few I'm thinking about, but I'm not sure I have the grades to get into all of them. My parents are getting on my case to make a decision, and I'm really stressed out about it. I'm not sure what to do."

Michael: "I can see why you're stressed over this. Picking a college is a big deal. Which ones are you thinking about?"

Riley: "Well, I'm not sure I want to go to college. I don't really like school, and college is expensive."

Michael: "That's true. What are you thinking about as a career or job? That might be a good place to start."

In this scenario, Riley is struggling with deciding about life after high school. She's not sure what steps to take to make the right decision, and it's causing her a lot of stress. Many people struggle, like Riley, with figuring out how to make decisions or solve problems in their lives. But giving up on solving a problem or putting off making a decision doesn't help. And people who don't know how to solve problems may be more likely to struggle with depression.

Problem-solving skills can be useful when helping someone or when trying to solve problems in your own life. And they're easy to teach and learn. This chapter shares some basic problem-solving skills you can teach to help someone right now and in the future.

# What Are Problem-Solving Skills?

Problem-solving is a skill you can use to identify a problem, figure out what is causing it, come up with possible solutions, pick the solution you think will work best, and try it out. All people use problem-solving skills every day, often without realizing it. If you tend to forget to bring your homework to school, you might decide to put it in your backpack before you go to bed—that's problem-solving. If you can't figure out a math problem and you ask a friend, parent, or teacher for help—problem-solving. If you want to make new friends, you might think about joining a club or sports team—problem-solving again.

Problem-solving skills are another set of tools you can use to help people, in addition to the basic helping skills and the solution-finding skills you learned about in chapters 4 and 5. You will likely need many of those skills when helping someone figure out what they want to do about a specific problem.

Here are some examples of common problems kids and teens have that they may need help in solving:

- wanting to make more friends
- feeling excluded or rejected
- having trouble falling asleep
- making decisions on how and when to do chores or homework
- choosing friends
- figuring out who to invite to a party or sleepover
- deciding whether to use drugs with friends
- determining what career they might like to pursue
- wanting to lose weight or get in shape
- eating a healthier diet
- deciding to break up with someone
- having difficulty ending screen time or choosing real life over screens
- dealing with issues at work
- resolving conflicts with friends or siblings
- having too many activities and extracurriculars,or not enough

Learning to solve problems probably doesn't sound like a "skill" at first. It might seem different from learning to shoot hoops, figuring out a math problem, or becoming a better artist or writer. But problem-solving *is* a skill you can learn and one you can help other people learn. Just remember that problems can take many forms. There isn't ever a right or wrong way to solve them, as long as no one gets hurt in the process. Learning some basic problem-solving skills—and practicing them regularly with the people you're helping—will also improve your ability to solve problems in your own life.

An important part of problem-solving is figuring out what is causing the problem. This can be hard. It's not always easy for people to look at themselves and figure out if they are doing something to contribute to or cause their problem. The good news is that if someone realizes, as a result of talking with you, that they are part of the problem, they may be more open to taking steps to fix their part. And taking steps to fix their part makes it more likely that the problem will be solved.

If someone's problem is with themselves, such as wanting to improve grades, remember to do chores, or decide what career to pursue, finding a good solution can lower stress and make the person happier. Whatever the problem, letting the person know that you are there to help can give them hope that they will figure out what they need to do.

## The Five Steps of Problem-Solving

It can help to think of problem-solving as having five steps. Here's one way to remember them: **IDEAL**.

**I** = **Identify** the problem.

**D** = **Define** the context of the problem. (When does it happen? What might be causing it?)

E = **Explore** possible strategies and the pros and cons of each.

A = **Act** on the solution you think is best.

L = **Look** back to see if your solution worked.

## IDENTIFY THE PROBLEM

The first step in solving a problem is to identify it—to give the problem a name. Usually, this is a simple sentence. Writing it (and the rest of these steps) can help, because it allows the person to focus on what exactly is the problem. Here are some examples:

- I can't decide on which classes to take next year.
- My grades are dropping, and I don't know how to fix them.
- My best friend doesn't invite me to her house anymore.
- I want to get along better with my brother.
- I want to get in better shape.
- I'm not sure if I still want to be friends with someone.
- I want a better relationship with my parents.
- I need to be more organized.
- I want to stop getting into fights with my girlfriend.

## DEFINE THE CONTEXT OF THE PROBLEM

In this second step, you assist the person in figuring out the *what* and *why* of the problem. You might ask questions such as:

- "Have you had this problem before?"
- "When does this problem occur? How often?"
- "What do you think might be causing this problem?"
- "What might be making this problem harder to solve?"
- "Are there times when the problem doesn't occur? What's different about those times?"

- "Do you think you might be contributing to the problem? If so, how?"

Understanding what may be contributing to the problem and why can help someone figure out solutions. Sometimes, it's easy to figure out what's behind a problem. Other times it is trickier if there are a number of things adding to the problem. Be sure to take some time on this step before moving on to step 3.

Here's an example of how you might help someone determine the context of their problem. Notice how, in this scenario, Jayse is trying to encourage Aria to explore the problem further and think of some solutions.

> **Aria:** "I'm so tired of getting into fights with my boyfriend. It's really getting to me and I'm not sure what to do about it."
>
> **Jayse:** "That sounds frustrating. Tell me a little more about it. What do you think might be causing the arguing?"

**Aria:** "Well, he gets upset if I'm out with friends and I don't respond to his texts."

**Jayse:** "Why do you think that bothers him so much?"

**Aria:** "I think maybe he feels left out or that I don't care enough about him to spend more time with him."

**Jayse:** "Hmmm. Have you asked him if that's how he feels?"

**Aria:** "Not yet, but I could try that. He usually just gets defensive when I ask why he's so upset."

**Jayse:** "Do you want to spend more time with him?"

**Aria:** "Kind of. I don't want to give up my friends though."

**Jayse:** "Sounds like a tough situation. What do you think you'll do?"

# EXPLORE POSSIBLE SOLUTIONS

The third problem-solving step is figuring out possible solutions. This is also called brainstorming, and you'll want to help the person come up with as many solutions as they can. Don't worry about how good the solutions are during this step, or how realistic. That's part of the fun! You can ask the person to write down the solutions they brainstorm or you can offer to keep a list for them.

Start by asking if they've thought of any ways that they might deal with the problem or if there's anyone else who might have ideas for how to solve it. It is important to first ask the person you're helping for ideas, since people are more likely to follow through when they figure out their own solutions.

You can offer to make some suggestions if the person is having trouble coming up with their own ideas. Be sure to ask first, though. If they say this is okay, then you can share your solutions. It is still up to them to accept or reject your suggestions. Try not to take it personally if they don't like your ideas. Remember, this is about them.

Here are a few examples of possible solutions to various problems, keeping in mind that some might not be good ones:

- I could take turns playing video games with my sister.
- I could get my chores done before I go out.
- I could set aside some time to study every day.
- I could sneak my phone into my room so I can talk to my friends at night.
- I could set up a time to talk with my friend about why they aren't inviting me over.
- I could meet with my school counselor to talk about my classes for next year.
- I could ask my uncle for advice on career choices.
- I could fail for the year and wait until next year to study for my tests.
- I could just end my friendship and ghost him.
- I could pack my backpack the night before so I don't forget to bring my stuff to school.
- I could write up a contract about my cell phone use and present it to my parents calmly.

Once the person has a list of possible solutions, talk about the pros and cons of each. Make a list with two columns, putting the pros on one side and cons on the other. After doing this, ask the person to cross out the solutions they know are definitely not good ideas. This should leave at least a few solutions to consider.

Here's a sample chart to show how this might look. This person wants to solve a problem of dropping grades.

| SOLUTIONS | PROS | CONS |
|---|---|---|
| study harder | grades would improve | less time for gaming or hanging out with friends |
| cheat my way through | grades might improve | I won't learn and I might get caught |
| study with a friend for tests | would be fun, grades might improve | I'd have to figure out how to get together with the friend |
| give up and don't worry about it | less stress | might fail the class |

## ACT ON A SOLUTION

Next, ask the person to pick one solution they are willing to try. Writing it can make them more committed to follow through. Encourage them to try the solution and express your faith in their ability to do it. This can motivate them to give it a try. Remind them that if the first solution doesn't work, they can always try a different one.

## LOOK BACK TO SEE IF IT WORKED

The last step of problem-solving, after trying out the solution, is to see if it worked the way the person wanted it to. It can help to set a time frame for trying before looking back. If someone agrees to try doing their homework before playing video games, suggest that they give it a few weeks to see if their grades improve. If it hasn't worked out so well after that time, they can always try a different solution that they didn't pick the first time. It also helps to encourage the person to try to figure out why the solution didn't work. That can give them clues that can help them pick a better solution.

# Goal Setting

Some problems can be solved by setting a goal and coming up with steps to achieve it. This works well for people who are having trouble with problems such as needing to study more, get more exercise, be nicer to their siblings, make more friends, be more responsible with chores, or eat a more nutritious diet.

You can help someone set a goal for these kinds of issues (or set one for yourself). Try using the following goal-setting prompts to help the person name and define their goal. Encourage them to write the prompts and their answers.

- What is my goal?
- Why is it important to me?
- What are some problems I might have in reaching my goal?
- What strengths do I have that will help me reach my goal?
- What steps will I take to reach my goal?
- When will I reach my goal?
- How can I reward myself once I reach my goal?

## GOAL SETTING IN ACTION

Here's an example of how this might work. Amir wants to get in better shape. He tried out for the cross country team last year and didn't make it because he couldn't keep up with the other runners. He realizes that he has to practice and probably give up some gaming, which takes up hours of his time. His friend Lena wants to help him figure out how to reach his goal. She helps Amir talk through the goal-setting prompts. Here are Amir's answers.

**What is my goal?** I want to increase my running speed so I can make the cross country team.

**Why is this goal important to me?** Lots of my friends are on the team, and I feel like I'm missing out on the fun. I have also been gaining weight and I don't feel that good about how I look. Plus my parents are always bugging me to eat healthier and get outside more.

**What are some problems I might have in reaching my goal?** I really like gaming and I have a lot of friends online. I know I should play less and practice more if I want to make the team, but it's a lot easier to game than it is to run.

**What strengths do I have that will help me reach my goal?** I know I can do it if I try. I brought up my grades last quarter, even though it took a lot of work. I also have a lot of friends on the team, and I think they'd help me train if I asked.

**What steps will I take to reach my goal?** Starting tomorrow, I'll go for a 15-minute run after school before I let myself start gaming. After a week, I'll run for 30 minutes before gaming. I'll also try to add speed intervals in my run, and I'll ask my friends to run with me, or if I can work out with them at the gym. They can help me stay on track. I will time my mile pace once a week. I'll also skip sugary breakfasts and have eggs or oatmeal instead. I could try eating more vegetables too—maybe!

**When will I reach my goal?** Tryouts for the cross country team are in two months.

**How can I reward myself when I reach my goal?** I think making the team would be a great reward! But a new game I want is coming out soon. I won't let myself buy it until I reach my goal.

Keep in mind that when you are helping someone set goals for themselves, you want to help them make sure their goals are reasonable and attainable. For example, bringing your grades up to straight A's after getting mostly Cs all year isn't very likely. Having reasonable and attainable goals help people follow through, since they are confident they can achieve them. Let them know that they can use the same goal-setting prompts with new goals and situations.

The tips in this chapter can aid you in helping people figure out why they are having a problem, find solutions, and set goals. But remember that you're not expected to know all the answers or even to come up with the solutions. You can't make a person do something to solve their problem, no matter how easy it might seem. That needs to come from the person themselves. But helping people in their search for answers can give them confidence to solve their problems and accountability to follow through.

## CHAPTER 7

# Teaching Conflict-Resolution Skills

**Ezra:** "Savannah and Wen, what brings you two in today, and how can I help?"

**Savannah:** "Wen and I got into a huge fight over some pictures I posted on Instagram."

**Wen:** "Yeah, she posted some pictures I told her not to post. I got a lot of negative comments about them."

**Savannah:** "You never told me I couldn't post them!"

**Wen:** "I did too! We were at your house when I told you not to!"

**Ezra:** "Sounds like you both are pretty upset with each other. Let's work together to see if we can resolve this so you can get back to being friends."

Conflict is a normal part of life. Disagreeing about an issue or behavior or arguing with friends and family can be stressful. Young people (and many adults) often don't know how to resolve conflict. No one really teaches them. Adults at home may tell kids to stop fighting or arguing, but this doesn't explain or show how to handle conflict. Conflicts at home and at school can lead to hurt feelings, broken friendships, and in severe cases, violence. This chapter shares some basic skills you can use to help people resolve conflict. You'll likely find them useful in your own life as well.

# Causes of Conflict

No two people are going to agree on everything. That would make life pretty dull! Often conflict stems from two (or more) people having different ideas of what they need and want. For example, you might want to hang out at the mall with friends, but your parents say you need to stay home to work on a school project or watch a younger sibling. Or maybe you want to participate in a pickup game after school, but it's already started and the kids who are playing don't want you to join in the middle.

Here are some common causes of conflict between young people. See which ones you can relate to.

- sharing secrets
- liking the same person
- spreading rumors
- disagreeing over the rules of a game
- a friend dating an ex
- taking turns when gaming
- borrowing things without asking
- teasing or name-calling
- gossiping
- sharing friends
- quitting a game when you're losing
- arguing with siblings
- dating partners feeling ignored or threatened by friends
- having contact with exes
- sharing passwords with friends or dating partners
- communicating effectively when having a disagreement

Often when people are in conflict, they raise their voices and start yelling at each other. They might call each other names, insult each other, or resort to physical violence. You can help people who are not getting along figure out healthy ways to resolve their differences and move forward.

Conflict resolution is similar to problem-solving in a lot of ways. But while problem-solving usually involves one person working to solve an issue or situation on their own, conflict resolution is about helping two or more people figure out how to resolve their disagreements. Sometimes, you can teach conflict-resolution skills to one person, which can help them talk with the person with whom they have a conflict.

Good solutions that resolve conflicts between people are often "win-win" solutions. This means that if two people are having a problem with each other, both need to feel good about the solution so they both feel they got something positive out of the process.

# Helping People Resolve Conflict

Conflict resolution is just as it sounds—helping people who are having a conflict or disagreement resolve their issues peacefully. When done right, the resolution can preserve a friendship or relationship.

Helping people deal with their differences can be tough. By the time people ask for help in resolving conflict, they are usually at a loss for what to do and can't seem to make any progress. They are likely feeling quite angry, and perhaps hurt as well. One important thing to remember when helping people resolve conflict is that once something hurtful is said, it can't be unsaid. Remind the people you're helping of this and ask them to choose their words carefully.

Usually people need to get to a calmer place, emotionally, before they are ready to resolve their conflict. Whenever you are helping people resolve conflict, no matter if they are friends, siblings, or other kids in your school, keep in mind these basic guidelines:

- Avoid taking sides.
- Help the people calm down.
- Encourage them to take a time-out if needed.
- Prepare them to listen to each other's point of view.
- Encourage them to take responsibility for their roles in the conflict.
- Help them take turns talking and avoid interrupting or speaking over each other.

- Help them express their feelings without being rude or disrespectful.
- See if they are willing to negotiate or compromise.

You'll need to use many of the basic helping skills you learned in chapter 4 to let the participants know you hear and understand their concerns and that you are there to help them come up with solutions they both can live with. Making eye contact, asking questions, reflecting feelings, restating, and summarizing what you hear them say are especially important. This helps both people calm down so that they are more open to seeing each other's point of view.

## KEEP IN MIND

In talking with people about their conflict, you might feel pressured to take one person's side over the other. This can be especially true if you're trying to help friends or teammates who are having a disagreement. You might even agree with one person over the other. But if you take a side, this will limit your ability to help and the people you're helping might lose trust in you. You might even get pulled into the argument.

So, notice if you're leaning toward one side, and do your best to stay neutral. Always remember that while you might be able to suggest some ways that people can handle their conflict, the decision to do so and the choice of what solution to try are up to them.

Like other skills, becoming good at resolving conflict takes time and practice. By teaching people how to resolve conflict peacefully, you are giving them skills that they can use to handle future conflicts on their own.

The following short videos can give you a brief idea of how conflict resolution works. If you like them, you can also share them with the people you're trying to help. Ask what they thought about the videos and if they'd be willing to try the suggestions.

- BrainPOP "Conflict Resolution": brainpop.com/health/ conflictresolution/conflictresolution
- AMAZE Org "Fighting Fair: How to Resolve Conflicts": youtu.be/gu8gSuF_lvw

## WHAT WE CAN LEARN FROM PIGS ABOUT CONFLICT RESOLUTION

Did you know that pigs, who are very social creatures, seem to be smart enough to know when to help deescalate a situation in the barnyard? This ability doesn't just help the pigs who are in conflict; it also helps the entire group. As part of a study led by Giada Cordoni, scientists observed that pigs who see a conflict happening will approach the fighting pigs and touch them with their snouts. This kind of touching is a common way pigs comfort each other. They will also rub the fighting pigs' ears or just sit near them. This behavior is also seen in groups of wolves, monkeys, and birds.

While people aren't pigs, we too benefit from physical connection. Sitting next to someone while giving them your full attention, laying a comforting hand on their shoulder, or offering a hug can provide comfort or help them settle down.

## THE IMPORTANCE OF I-MESSAGES

When two people are in conflict, they often accuse each other of starting the problem. "*You* made *me* angry!" "*You* took *my* phone without asking!" The problem with this approach is that the other person gets defensive and usually argues back: "I did not!" "It's *your* fault for not messaging *me* back for hours!"

I-messages are a way to avoid this cycle of accusation and defensiveness. By starting with *I*, someone is sharing how they feel and not blaming the other person. It's harder to argue with feelings, since feelings belong to an individual—they are what they are. I-messages also make it easier for everyone to stay calm. Follow this format when teaching others to use I-messages, and follow it yourself:

I feel (or I felt)____ when you ____ because ____. I want ____.

Here's a trick to remember it. Try saying the following line with a bouncy rhythm to help it stick in your head: **I feel, when you, because, I want.**

Here's an example of an I-message in action:

> "Jesse, **I feel** upset **when you** tease me in front of my friends **because** it embarrasses me. **I want** you to stop doing that."

I-messages are also useful when explaining feelings about something that happened in the past:

> "Tanisha, **I felt** really hurt **when you** had a party at your house and you didn't invite me **because** I thought we were better friends. I saw all the pictures online. **I want** to know why you didn't invite me."

Knowing how and when to use I-messages is a skill that will prove valuable in many situations. When you're helping people in conflict, you can share these examples to guide them to use I-messages. Teaching people this technique can help them strengthen their relationships and resolve hurt feelings in a constructive way.

## REFLECTIVE LISTENING AND SUMMARIZING IN CONFLICT RESOLUTION

When people are in conflict, they often spend more time trying to get their point across than listening to why the other person is upset and attempting to see things from a different point of view. This usually heats up the argument and can lead to yelling and repetition—both unhelpful in resolving the conflict.

To figure out a win-win solution, it's much better if people try to listen more than they talk. One way of doing this is to use reflective listening, a skill you learned about in chapter 4. This involves repeating back what another person said so they know you are trying to understand. Recall the conflict between Savannah and Wen. Here's an example of how Ezra might use reflective listening to help Savannah and Wen understand each other:

> "Wen, you're saying you felt really upset and hurt when Savannah posted pictures after you asked her not to. And then you got a lot of negative comments about them. Savannah, you don't remember Wen asking you not to post the pictures, and now you're not sure why he's upset. Is that right?"

Reflective listening slows down the conversation and helps people stay calm. When you are trying to help people in conflict, encourage them to use reflective listening when discussing the problem and repeat back what they hear one another say. You can model for them how to do this by repeating back what you hear each person saying.

Reflective listening is a skill you'll use often when helping people resolve conflict, and it's a good skill to have for conflicts that arise in your life too. You can try using it when someone is mad at you.

# PEER COUNSELOR TIP

## Conflict Resolution and Peer Mediation

While helping friends or classmates resolve conflict is something anyone can do, some schools have a specific program for this called peer mediation. During the mediation process, a student (or pair of students) trained in peer mediation listens to the people who are in conflict. They allow each person to present their side of a disagreement and help them find a way to resolve their differences. Participating in peer mediation is generally voluntary. Students can choose not to participate. But if a disciplinary action is part of the issue, school officials may agree to hold off on it if both people agree to peer mediation. This gives students more reason to try it.

Participating in peer mediation teaches the mediators as well as the students in mediation basic communication skills that can not only help them resolve differences, but also help them in other situations in life since the same skills used for conflict resolution are used in peer mediation. The process is very similar.

Peer mediation can't help with all situations. For example, if the situation involves physical aggression or sexual assault, or if weapons or drugs are part of the dispute, adults need to be involved to keep everyone safe.

# Stages of Conflict Resolution

As with problem-solving, think of conflict resolution as occurring in stages. The stages are pretty much the same whether you are helping people resolve conflicts in a formal or informal way, though the introduction and closing stages apply mostly to formal peer mediation. The stages are:

1. Introduction and overview
2. Each person gives their side
3. Reflection/restatement of each side
4. Summary of the problem
5. Brainstorm of possible solutions
6. Agreement on a solution
7. Session closing

Some people you help will need to work through all the stages. Others may skip around and come up with solutions more quickly. Always let the people in conflict lead the process.

## INTRODUCTION AND OVERVIEW

This step is mostly for peer counselors and mediators. Whenever you start a conflict resolution or peer mediation session, giving a brief introduction and overview of the process is important. Here's an example:

> "Welcome! My name is ____ and I'm here to help you identify the issues between you, understand each other's feelings and positions better, and come up with a solution that works for everyone. I'm not here to tell you what to do, but I will help you stay on track and be respectful toward each other. What we talk about will stay private unless you share information that could put someone in danger, such as a threat or a weapon. If that happens, we'll need to talk with adults to figure out how to best help you and keep everyone safe. Do you have any questions before we start?"

As part of your overview, it is important to ask the participants to agree to some basic rules (see the next Peer Counselor Tip). This makes it more likely that the session will stay respectful and be productive. You will likely have to remind them of the rules during the session, too, as things can get heated. Use a calm voice when asking them not to interrupt, to lower their voice, or to stay quiet while the other person is talking. Let them know you will interrupt them and ask them to stop if needed.

## PEER COUNSELOR TIP
### Rules for Mediating Conflict

1. Share these rules when you're helping people resolve conflicts.

2. Don't interrupt—let the other person speak.

3. No cussing—that can make people angrier.

4. Choose your words carefully—this helps the other person listen to your side.

5. No name-calling or put-downs—keep it respectful.

6. As you listen, try to see it from the other person's point of view.

## EACH PERSON GIVES THEIR SIDE

In this stage, each person is asked to explain their side of what happened or what the issue is. If you're not a peer counselor or peer mediator and skip the introduction, this would be where you start. You can ask some of the following questions to help you understand the conflict and what people want to happen:

- "How do you know each other?"
- "Have you had this kind of conflict before?"
- "How would you like this session to go?"
- "Is there anything you'd like me to know before we start?"

Then invite the people to state, one at a time, the conflict or problem from their point of view. Once everyone has given their side, you can move them to reflecting and restating what was said.

## REFLECTION/RESTATEMENT OF EACH SIDE

In this stage, you will ask the people in conflict to really talk to each other. They've had a chance to hear each other's point of view; now they need to reflect what they heard. Use reflective listening to let each person know that you heard them correctly. Ask them to restate to each other what they heard. This way, they are practicing the skill with each other. But if things get too heated, you can be the one to reflect.

## SUMMARY OF THE PROBLEM

Once both people have had a chance to state their side and reflect what they heard from each other, you can summarize your understanding of the problem, giving both sides. When people are in conflict, it can help them to hear the conflict from an outside point of view as a way of understanding both sides. Summarizing also reinforces that you heard everyone correctly. Here's an example:

> "So, Sacha, you're upset because you told Keiko about your boyfriend's problems in confidence. You thought she understood not to share it with anyone and now your

boyfriend is upset because he heard about what you shared from one of his friends. Is that right?"

"Keiko, you don't remember Sacha saying anything about keeping it private and now you feel really bad about sharing what he told you. If you had realized it, you would never have said something. Did I miss anything?"

## BRAINSTORM OF POSSIBLE SOLUTIONS

During this stage, you will help people in conflict brainstorm possible solutions. Sometimes, this is as simple as making a promise to each other not to repeat a behavior that was hurtful. For others, brainstorming to come up with ways to resolve an argument can be helpful in discovering the root of the conflict and finding a solution that everyone is happy about. If people are having a hard time coming up with a solution, you can ask if they are open to your suggestions. If they are, share your ideas.

## AGREEMENT ON A SOLUTION

Once participants have brainstormed solutions, they need to agree on a solution to try. If you have helped them write a list of possible solutions, they can cross out the ones that definitely won't work and focus on a few that might. Here are some questions you can ask to help them along:

- "Which of these solutions look good to you?"
- "Which solutions are you willing to try?"
- "What are some advantages of trying this solution first?"
- "Would you like to pick a back-up solution in case the first one doesn't work?"
- "How can I help you both come up with a solution that might work?"

You can also use a chart similar to the one on page 85 to help them list the pros and cons of each possible solution.

## SESSION CLOSING

If you're helping people resolve conflicts as a peer counselor or peer mediator, you'll want to close the mediation session once they come up with a solution. It's helpful to encourage them to say something positive to each other as a good ending. Here are some examples:

- "Thanks for agreeing to meet with me. It was helpful!"
- "I accept your apology."
- "I'm sorry for hurting your feelings. I will try to do better in the future."

Shaking hands or hugging at the end might also be appropriate, if all participants are comfortable with it and want to do so. Hugging can be especially helpful if all of you are friends, as it can make it clear that you're okay with each other and back to being friends.

You can also ask for feedback on how things went:

- "What do you both think of how this went today?"
- "What was most helpful?"
- "Was there anything I said or did that wasn't so helpful?"
- "What could you do differently if this problem happens again?"

# Helping with Conflict Resolution When Only One Person Is Present

Sometimes, a person may come to you with an issue involving another person who is not present. A common example might be someone who is having an issue with a parent or another adult in their life. Even though you won't be mediating the conflict, you can still help the person learn conflict-resolution skills and how to approach the other person. It is often true that the way in which you approach another person affects how open they are to what you have to say. Consider this scenario:

Finn wants a later curfew, but their grandma always tells them no and this leads to an argument.

One of the best ways of approaching parents, grandparents, or other adults at home is to ask questions that start with *what would it take*, *what do you think*, or *would you be willing*.

Here are a few questions Finn might use:

- **"What would it take** for you to consider giving me a later curfew?"
- **"Would you be willing** to extend my curfew this Friday so I can go to a birthday party for my friend?"
- **"What do you think** about giving me a later curfew?"

In a different scenario, Daniel wants his parents to back off on his grades. He has a hard time keeping up with his schoolwork, but having his parents yell at him or ground him just makes him angry and less willing to try. Here are some ways he might bring it up to them:

- "I know my grades aren't the greatest and I want to do better. But it just makes me mad when you yell at me. I have a proposal. **Would you be willing** to let me handle my grades this quarter and if I drop below a B, you can help me during the next quarter?"
- "I know I need to get my homework done after school, but I need some chill time first. **What do you think** about letting me have an hour of gaming time before I start my homework?"

These are all respectful ways Finn and Daniel can ask for what they want to solve a problem. But's it's not just how or what someone asks. Tone of voice is also very important. An angry, demanding tone usually results in a negative reaction from the other person.

One strategy for helping people be more respectful and calmer in their approach is to suggest a role-play scenario, with you taking the role of the absent person and the person you're helping playing themselves. They can practice sharing I-messages and asking for what they want, and you can give feedback on their tone and approach. You can also demonstrate a tone you think might be more helpful, and invite the person to try the role-play again.

The suggestions in this chapter are a great start to helping people work out conflicts with one another. If you'd like to learn more about helping people resolve conflict, the following resources may be helpful:

- "Facts for Teens: Conflict Resolution" by the National Youth Violence Prevention Resource Center: web.njit.edu/~lipuma/Conflict.pdf
- "Conflict Resolution for Teens: 9 Essential Skills" by Mat Woods: teenwire.org/conflict-resolution-for-teens
- *The Mindful Guide to Conflict Resolution: How to Thoughtfully Handle Difficult Situations, Conversations, and Personalities* by Rosalie Puiman

## CHAPTER 8

# When to Seek Adult Help

**Jen:** "This school year has really sucked. Most of my friends don't want to be around me, and my parents are always bugging me."

**Eddy:** "That sounds pretty awful. Not getting along with friends and family is really stressful."

**Jen:** "Yeah, they just don't get it. Sometimes, it feels like it's just not worth living anymore."

**Eddy:** "I can understand that. When you say it's not worth living anymore, are you thinking about hurting or killing yourself?"

**Jen:** "Sometimes. I don't think I'd really do it, but maybe, if things don't get better."

While most of the time when helping others you'll hear about everyday situations and stressors, you might also hear stories like the one above. Self-harm, suicidal thoughts and plans, and other high-risk situations you might hear about are not issues you can take on alone. And you are never expected to be an expert or to have solutions to these kinds of problems. When they come up, you need to tell an adult you trust (or your peer supervisor, if you are working as a peer counselor) right away.

This chapter is not meant to scare you, but it is important information to learn. Knowing which situations need adult intervention and what questions to ask in the moment can help people stay safe and find the help they need.

# Suicidal Thoughts and Plans

Death by suicide is a serious problem worldwide. In the United States alone, about 46,000 people died by suicide in 2020. It is the third leading cause of death in young people ages 10–19, and the rates of death are increasing. In 2019, about 14 out of every 100,000 people ages 15–24 died by suicide. More teens are killing themselves using a weapon compared to years past. A survey by the CDC found that lesbian, gay, and bisexual high school students are three times as likely to consider suicide compared to their heterosexual peers, and five times as likely to attempt it. A survey conducted by the Trevor Project in 2022 found that 45 percent of LGBTQ+ adolescents ages 13 to 24 considered suicide in the last year and almost 1 in 5 transgender and nonbinary adolescents attempted suicide.

Suicidal thoughts are also common among teens and young adults. According to the CDC report, close to 20 percent of high school students report serious thoughts about suicide and 9 percent report a suicide attempt. This means that the chances are pretty high that you will hear from someone who has thought about suicide.

Even younger kids think about and attempt suicide. Researchers at Oregon Health & Science University found that the number of kids who have overdosed on drugs or other dangerous chemicals in an attempt to kill themselves has increased significantly in the last ten years, from 1,058 in 2010 to 5,606 in 2020. That's five times as many kids. The Covid-19 pandemic has added to this number. Many of these cases could be prevented if kids and teens could get professional help, though that doesn't always help everyone.

Hearing about suicidal thoughts or plans is very scary. You can expect to feel nervous if someone tells you they want to hurt or kill themselves. If someone tells you about suicidal thoughts or plans, let them know you will need to share this with an adult right away. You can also share hotlines that are available for people thinking about suicide. In the United States, you can call or text 988 or chat 988lifeline. org to reach the 988 Suicide & Crisis Lifeline. LGBTQ+ kids and teens can also speak to a crisis

988 SUICIDE & CRISIS LIFELINE
text or call: 988
chat: 988lifeline.org

THE TREVOR PROJECT
call: 1-866-488-7386
text: "START" to 678-678
chat: thetrevorproject.org

counselor at the Trevor Project. To reach a live person, call 1-866-488-7386, text "START" to 678-678, or chat online. Keep this information handy so you can share it with people in the moment. Suggest that they put the number in their phone so they won't have to search for it if they need it.

When talking with people about feelings and problems, don't ever hesitate to ask if they are having suicidal thoughts, especially if they tell you that they are feeling sad or depressed. Asking does not "give them the idea" if they weren't already thinking about it, and it can help them get the support they need when you share the issue with an adult. Here are some ways you can ask:

- "Are you having any suicidal thoughts?"
- "Have you come up with a plan on how you would kill yourself?"
- "Do you think you might act on those thoughts?"
- "What has kept you from acting on those thoughts before?"

Share their answers with an adult or your peer counseling supervisor right away.

# Nonsuicidal Self-Injury or Self-Harm

For some kids and teens, self-harm is a way of relieving emotional pain, since feeling physical pain can distract people from their emotional pain. This might take the form of cutting, burning, biting, or scratching. For most people, self-harm isn't about wanting to die. Instead, it is a way of staying alive by making emotional pain more tolerable, at least temporarily. It can also be a way of expressing anger at oneself or at someone else who might be upset about the injuries. Often, people cover their injuries by wearing long sleeves or pants or injuring in places on their bodies that others can't see.

One problem with this is that self-injury can be addictive and can progress from small injuries to repeated, more serious, or deeper injuries that can cause permanent damage and scarring. It can bring temporary relief but is often followed by feelings of guilt or shame. Using self-injury as a main coping strategy can keep people from learning healthier ways of coping. It can also endanger their life if they cut too deep.

If you are helping someone who shares that they are engaging in self-harm, ask these questions:
- "How often are you self-harming?"
- "How do you feel before and after you do it?"
- "Do you think it helps? Does it ever make you feel worse?"
- "Are there other things you can do to feel better instead of self-injuring?"
- "Is self-harming something that you want to stop?"

Given the possible risks of self-injury, this is also something that you should share with a trusted adult or peer supervisor. You can also share these resources: S.A.F.E. Alternatives (selfinjury.com, 1-800-366-8288) and The Mighty: (themighty.com/topic/self-harm/what-is-self-harm).

# Homicidal Thoughts and Plans

Everyone gets angry sometimes. Getting upset at being teased, getting bad grades, being embarrassed in front of others, being rejected by friends or dating partners, and getting in trouble with adults are all common triggers of frustration and anger. Usually, the feeling passes quickly and you get over it. However, some teens can't stop thinking about it, and they seriously consider expressing their anger aggressively by hurting others. Being murdered is now one of the most frequent causes of death among teens.

In the United States, school shootings have been and continue to be an urgent problem. They are incredibly traumatic, and too many students have witnessed school shootings or been affected by them. They are still rare, though, and your chances of being a victim of one are generally low.

Most school shooters are white males. Many have been bullied or abused, and most have felt rejected by peers. Often, there are warning signs. They may "joke" about shooting up a school or post violent images or thoughts online. They might brag about having weapons or show them off to their friends. Sometimes, no one really knows how troubled or serious a shooter is until it is too late. This is why it is crucial that you tell an adult or peer counseling supervisor *whenever* anyone tells you about homicidal or violent thoughts or plans.

If you are concerned about someone's anger, and you feel safe doing so, you might ask a few questions, but a professional should really be the one to talk with the person about these kinds of thoughts.

- "Have you thought about hurting someone on purpose?"
- "Have you thought of killing someone lately?"
- "If so, how are you thinking of doing it?"
- "Do you think you might actually do it? Are you planning on killing someone?"
- "What do you think might happen if you do?"
- "What has kept you from acting on these thoughts already?"
- "What are some ways you can vent your anger that won't hurt anyone else?"
- "Would you like some ideas on how to handle your anger?"

If you ever hear someone talking about killing others, tell an adult immediately. This is true even if the person you are worried about is a friend or family member. If no one listens to you, call 911 and report what you heard. It is better to be wrong than to wish you had said something after a tragedy occurs.

# Alcohol and Drug Use

Use of alcohol and drugs among teens is common. Chances are that you or someone you know has tried alcohol, experimented with drugs, or smoked or vaped. For most people, this doesn't cause major problems. However, for some, using drugs or alcohol as a teen can lead to a lifelong struggle with addiction.

As a young person, you are not trained to figure out who is at greater risk for addiction. Just because someone tells you that they had a few beers at a party over the weekend doesn't mean you should report them to caregivers or school officials. But it may be helpful to ask more questions if you're concerned about someone's use to help you in making that decision. If the drug or alcohol use causes problems, interferes with their functioning, or gets them in trouble, chances are they have a substance use disorder. An easy way to remember how to ask about substance use is to use the acronym **CAGE**:

C: Do you ever feel you should **cut down** on your use?

A: Have you felt **annoyed by others** who are concerned about your use?

G: Have you ever felt **guilty** about your use?

E: Have you ever used in the morning, as an **"eye opener,"** to get rid of the effects of using the night before?

If you're concerned about someone's use, you can offer to share information about the risks of drugs and alcohol. You can encourage them to talk with their caregivers or other adults about getting professional help. Some schools have drug counselors. Students can refer themselves if they are willing to get help. Let them know that you are not trained to help with addiction problems.

If a friend tells you about their use and it concerns you, you might be worried that you'll come across as a "goody-goody" if you talk to them about the dangers of drugs or alcohol. And it is true that some teens can use drugs or alcohol without it causing problems, at least not at first. Here are some ways to show your concern without being preachy.

- "I'm really worried about what you're telling me. Smoking weed on occasion is one thing. But trying fentanyl can kill you. Can we talk about this?"
- "I'm really glad you told me about how much you drank at the party. But it scares me to death to hear that you drove home after that."

Since behaviors like these are extremely risky and can lead to death, telling an adult is needed. You can offer to help your friend talk to someone about it, whether that person is a parent, a school counselor, or another trusted adult. You may be afraid of upsetting your friend or having your friend decide that they don't want to be friends anymore. This can happen. But not doing anything and having something tragic happen is much worse. If this person is truly your friend, they may eventually forgive you and even thank you for caring enough to help them.

# Physical, Sexual, or Emotional Abuse

**Abdi:** "What's up, Sean? Haven't seen you around school in a while."

**Sean:** "It's nothing. Well, actually, things aren't going so well at home."

**Abdi:** "Sorry to hear that. Want to talk about it?"

**Sean:** "It's my dad. He's been drinking a lot lately. He gets really mad when he drinks, and I have to be there to protect my little brother. He acts up a lot."

**Abdi:** "Is your dad hurting your brother?"

**Sean:** "Sometimes. He goes after him with a belt, and I can hear my brother screaming. I've seen some purple bruises on his leg from getting hit."

**Abdi:** "That's not okay. Sounds like you're afraid something really bad might happen. Let's see if we can figure out what to do about it."

A peer you're talking with may share that they or someone they know has been or is being abused. This abuse can be by parents, siblings, other kids or adults, coaches, religious leaders, or dating partners. This is a really tough situation to hear about and it can be hard to know what to say or do. Professional therapists struggle with this too.

Physical abuse occurs when the abuser hits or strikes someone with fists, belts, sticks, or other items. It often leaves a bruise, which is one way to tell that the behavior is abusive. Spanking a child may or may not count as abuse. In some states, parents are allowed to spank their children for misbehavior. However, they are not allowed to hit so hard as to leave bruises or red marks.

Sexual abuse is when someone forces or coerces another person into performing sexual acts. This includes when the abuser touches a person in places on their body considered to be private areas, such as the chest, genitals, or buttocks, or makes the person touch them in similar ways. Another form of sexual abuse happens online, when predators ask kids or teens to send revealing pictures or videos of themselves. Some predators even offer money for these kinds of images, and then will threaten to expose the person or share the pictures and videos if they tell anyone what is happening.

Emotional abuse is when someone says mean and hurtful things to another person in a way that makes them feel bad about themselves. It can range from cussing at them, to putting them down, to saying things such as that they wished the person were never born. This kind of abuse is harder to deal with, as it's hard to draw the line between bad behavior and abusive behavior. Still, people who abuse others emotionally can damage their victims' self-esteem and lead to problems with depression and anger.

People who are abused are more likely to attempt suicide or use drugs or alcohol, often to try to deal with the emotions that come with being abused. It is also possible that the abuser has other victims. This is why reporting any kind of abuse is so important.

Here are some questions you can ask if you think someone you're helping is being abused:

- "Are you afraid of anyone in your life?"
- "What happens in your family when people get angry?"
- "What do adults in your home do when they get angry at you?"

- "Do people in your house hit others? When does that happen? How often?"
- "Have you ever been hurt by someone taking care of you?"
- "Has anyone ever touched you in a way you don't like?"
- "Is anyone making you do things you are uncomfortable or embarrassed to do?"

If someone you are helping tells you they are being abused, you *always* need to tell a trusted adult. This can be a parent, a school counselor, a therapist, a family doctor, or your school principal. Some adults are known as mandated reporters. This means they are required by law to report certain kinds of abuse to authorities who can investigate and help. If the first adult you tell doesn't believe you or does not report it, ask another adult for help. You can call or text the Childhelp National Child Abuse Hotline at 1-800-422-4453. You can also call your local police department and ask them about making a report. Don't give up until you find someone who is willing to take action.

In the United States, the authorities who investigate abuse are called different things in different counties or states. Child Protective Services or the Department of Family Services are two common names. Once abuse is reported, an investigator will usually visit the person, often at their school, to get more information. The abuser can be charged with a crime and if so will have to appear in court. Punishment can include jail time and/or being required to attend counseling or anger-management classes.

Be sure you have a plan ahead of time for who to report to if anyone you are helping is being abused. Making a list of people you can call is a good idea. If you are working in a peer counseling program, ask your supervisor what steps you need to take if this issue comes up. If you are trying to help a friend, you can talk to your parents, another trusted adult, or a school counselor about what to do.

## BULLYING

Bullying is another type of abuse. It is when a person or group intentionally threatens or hurts someone else, usually a stronger or more popular person bullying someone who is weaker or less popular. People bully for various reasons. They might want to make the other person feel bad, prove that they are tough, or control the other person and make them fearful. Bullying can take the form of physical violence or threats, teasing or making fun of someone, making inappropriate sexual comments, spreading rumors, trying to exclude someone by telling others not to be friends with them, or saying hurtful things. Embarrassing someone in front of others is another form of bullying. Cyberbullying is when the bullying is done online, such as through texting or social media. Taking a video of someone being attacked and posting it online or sharing it with friends is another type of cyberbullying. In some cases, kids who post about feeling depressed have been cyberbullied and told to kill themselves.

Bullying often happens away from adults who can stop it. It might happen in school hallways or bathrooms, outside at recess or on school grounds, or on the bus. About 20 percent of kids (one in five) report having been bullied. Kids who are bullied are more likely to become anxious or depressed. Some become suicidal.

If someone you are helping shares with you that they are being bullied, you can encourage them to let school authorities know, if it is happening at school. If it is happening outside of school, you can talk to your parents or other adults about it. They may be able to contact the parents of the person being bullied. You could offer to go with the targeted person to report the bullying if it would help.

You can also share anti-bullying resources. The Stop Bullying website (stopbullying.gov) has information on what to do if you think school staff are not taking complaints about bullying seriously enough. It also has a Youth Engagement Toolkit you can use if you want to do more about handling or preventing bullying in your school or area. The TeensHealth website (teenshealth.org/en/teens/bullies) also has resources you can share.

Kids and teens who are LBGTQ+ are at higher risk of bullying. And there are many resources specially for LGBTQ+ teens that you can share. Examples include:

- In the United States: call the Trevor Project at 1-866-488-7386
- In the United Kingdom: call Galop at 020 7704 2040
- In Canada: call LGBT Youth helpline at 1-800-268-9688
- In Australia: call QLife at 1800 184 527
- In India: call iCall at 9152987821

Bullying is a serious problem that can cause long-lasting damage to the person being bullied. Often kids and teens are afraid to come forward because they think it won't help. They worry that they won't be believed or that they'll be told to "just ignore it," which doesn't make the bullying any better. Letting people know that there is help for bullying can make a big difference in their lives.

# Other Risky Behaviors

Young people are known risk-takers. When you're young, you might think that bad things won't happen or that you won't get caught. But risky behaviors such as speeding, gambling too much, driving after drinking, or having sex with multiple partners can all cause serious problems.

Again, you are not a trained professional. When you hear about risky behaviors, you can encourage people to think about the pros and cons of their behavior to help them decide whether they need to make a change. You should also talk with an adult in these cases.

# Talking to Trusted Adults

Risky situations such as these are the hardest part of trying to help others and keep them safe. And they're stressful for you and the people you are helping. You might think that you need to keep these things private, especially if a friend asks you not to tell. But because these situations are so risky and can end up with people being harmed or killed, you must tell an adult about them right away. An adult will advise you on what to do or can take over themselves. This is especially important if someone tells you that they are planning to do something harmful now or in the near future. If you can't reach any trusted adults right away, you can always call 911. Tell the person what you know, and they will take it from there. Usually, they will send people who are trained to help in these situations. Sitting with the person who needs help during this process can make it easier for them to get through it.

If you are reading this book so you can help friends and family, you should also think about who you can go to if your friend or family member tells you something that is dangerous or too hard to handle on your own. Going to your parents first makes sense if it is someone in your family who is having trouble, perhaps with suicidal thoughts, driving drunk, wanting or planning on hurting or killing someone, or out-of-control drug use that could be deadly. If it is someone in school, talking with your school counselor or social worker is a wise choice.

# A Final Word

Helping others with their problems can be a difficult task. You might feel overwhelmed at times when listening to people's struggles. In the moment, it can seem like things will never get better.

The fact is that if a person has someone to talk with, who will listen and offer a sympathetic ear, and who can help them figure out how to cope and come up with solutions to problems, this makes all the difference in the world.

Helping others is an act of kindness that can make your world a better place. By learning the skills described in this book and sharing them with others, you can have a positive impact on the lives of friends, family members, and peers, as well as on your larger school and community. And you'll learn skills to help yourself as well!

# RESOURCES

## HELPING SKILLS

*Helping Skills: Facilitating Exploration, Insight, and Action*, fifth edition, **by Clara E. Hill.** Washington, DC: American Psychological Association.

*Peer Power, Book One: Workbook: Becoming an Effective Peer Helper and Conflict Mediator* **by Judith A. Tindall.** New York: Routledge.

## PEER MEDIATION AND CONFLICT RESOLUTION RESOURCES

**"10 Lessons for Teaching Conflict Resolution Skills" by Fairfax County Public Schools.** creducation.net/resources/CR_Guidelines_and_10_CR_lessons_FCPS.pdf.

*The Kids' Guide to Working Out Conflicts* **by Naomi Drew.** Minneapolis, MN: Free Spirit Publishing.

*New Jersey State Bar Foundation Peer Mediation Guide.* njsbf.org/school-based-programs/violence-preventionanti-bias-trainings/peer-mediation.

**"Peer Mediation" by EJHSCOLTS.** youtube.com/watch?v=q8TzOfT9d9k.

**"Peer Mediation 2018 Advisory Video" by Woburn Public Media Center.** youtube.com/watch?v=G4q1Qpt4iHA.

**"Peer Mediators" by Justin Nipp.** youtube.com/watch?v=PxCLtFWB74E.

*Resolving Conflict with a Peer Mediation Program* **by Maureen F. Block and Barbara Blazej.** umaine.edu/peace/wp-content/uploads/sites/173/2016/03/PEER_MEDIATION_FINAL_11.pdf.

## MENTAL HEALTH AND ADDICTION RESOURCES

**"67 Positive Affirmations for Teens & Younger Students" by Happier Human.** happierhuman.com/positive-affirmations-teens.

**Children of Parents with a Mental Illness.** copmi.net.au. This Australian website offers online resources explaining a parent's mental illness to children.

**Inside the Teenage Brain.** pbs.org.wgbh/pages/frontline/shows/teenbrain. This PBS program explains how the teenage brain operates.

**KidsHealth.** kidshealth.org. The website contains information on many mental health topics, with sections for kids and teens.

**Media and Body Image.** admedia.com/media-and-body-image.php. Aimed at women, this page addresses concerns about body image and the effects of media on body image issues. It includes tips for coping.

**The Mighty's Guide to Understanding Self-Harm.** themighty.com/topic/self-harm/what-is-self-harm. This page shares resources for people who self-injure or self-harm.

**National Institute on Drug Abuse.** nida.nih.gov. NIDA provides information and resources for helping those with addictions.

**Now Matters Now.** nowmattersnow.org. This is an online resource that provides support for coping with suicidal thoughts through teaching skills based on dialectical behavioral therapy (DBT). It includes videos of personal stories.

**Planned Parenthood.** plannedparenthood.org/learn/teens. This organization provides sexual and reproductive health services and education to people in need, including teens.

**RecoverYourLife.** recoveryourlife.com. This is a support community for kids and teens who self-injure.

**Society for the Prevention of Teen Suicide.** sptsusa.org/teens. This website has a teen section where you can find information to help yourself or a friend who may be having suicidal thoughts. You can also find information on how to cope if a friend dies by suicide.

**Teens Against Bullying.** pacerteensagainstbullying.org. This site was created by and for teens. It is a place for middle and high school students to find ways to address bullying, take action, be heard, and own an important social cause.

**Teen Help.** teenhelp.com. This website offers resources and information on specific topics related to mental health and general teen development and growth.

**YHELP! Youth Services.** yhelpnow.com. This youth platform for teens has content about mental health awareness, entertainment, and life.

**Youth Engaged 4 Change.** engage.youth.gov. This site provides youth-focused resources and opportunities that inspire and empower young people to make a difference in their lives and in the world around them by improving their knowledge and leadership skills. You can search opportunities to get involved, answers to questions you care about, and inspiration from others who have made a difference.

## MENTAL HEALTH AND ADDICTION RESOURCES (CONTINUED)

**Youth Motivating Others Through Voices of Experience** (Youth M.O.V.E. National). youthmovenational.org. This is a youth- and young-adult-led national advocacy organization that is devoted to improving services and systems that support young people. They focus on empowering young people to partner with adults to create meaningful change in mental health, juvenile justice, education, and child welfare systems.

## MENTORING RESOURCES

*High School Teen Mentoring Activity Book.* https://albertamentors.ca/wp-content/uploads/2013/10/MentoringActivityBookpdf.pdf.

**National Mentoring Resource Center.** nationalmentoringresourcecenter.org.

*Ongoing Training for Mentors* **edited by Amy Cannata.** educationnorthwest.org/sites/default/files/resources/Ongoing%20Training%20for%20Mentors.pdf.

*Peer Mentoring Guide* **by National Mentoring Resource Center.** ojjdp.ojp.gov/publications/peer-mentoring-guide.

## CRISIS HOTLINES

**Covenant House/National Runaway Safeline.** 1800runaway.org. Call 800-786-2929. Press 2 for crisis line; 3 for resources. This is a 24-hour confidential crisis and resource line for at-risk teens considering running away from home.

**National Alliance on Mental Illness.** nami.org/help. Call the NAMI Helpline at 800-950-6264. Text "HelpLine" to 62640. NAMI is a free, nationwide peer-support service providing information, resource referrals, and support to people living with a mental health condition, their family members and caregivers, mental health providers, and the public. The teen site (nami.org/your-journey/kids-teens-and-young-adults/teens) gives information on finding help, advice for talking to friends or parents about mental health issues including your own, how social media can affect mental health, and what to do if your mental health interferes with your academics or other school-related activities.

**National Safe Place.** nationalsafeplace.org. This is a 24-hour service that provides information, immediate help, and supportive resources for youth in need. Their website and text line include a "Find a Safe Place Locator" for teens in a crisis. Use TXT 4 HELP: text the word *safe* and your current location (city/state/zip) to 4HELP (44357).

**S.A.F.E. Alternatives.** selfinjury.com. Call 800-366-8288.

**Teen Line.** teenlineonline.org. Call 800-852-8336 or text TEEN to 839863. This teen hotline provides emotional support and education on common crises or issues to teens via phone, text, chat, email, and message boards. It also includes a parent and resource section with blogs and videos. Calls and texts answered between 6 p.m. and 10 p.m. PT.

**Thursday's Child.** thursdayschild.org. Call 800-872-5437. This line provides 24-hour emergency help and information for youths in crisis And helps children, teens and young adults faced with bullying, eating disorders, self-harm, sexual assault, thoughts of suicide, trafficking, abuse, abduction, and addiction.

**Your Life Your Voice** from Boys Town Hotline. yourlifeyourvoice.org. For preteens, teens, and young adults who are in crisis or feeling overwhelmed, Your Life Your Voice provides a toll-free, 24-hour hotline. You can call, text, chat, or email. Call 800-448-3000 or text "VOICE" to 20121. The website also has information sheets with tips for handling difficult situations, including an interactive list and print-out of 99 coping skills and strategies.

# LGBTQ+ RESOURCES

**It Gets Better Project.** itgetsbetter.org. Their mission is to uplift, empower, and connect LGBTQ+ young people around the globe. The website features videos of people of all ages describing their experiences.

**Trevor Project.** thetrevorproject.org. The Trevor Project provides suicide prevention and crisis intervention services to LGBTQ+ young people. It offers free, 24-7 confidential counseling through the following: Trevor Lifeline—toll-free phone line at 866-488-7386; TrevorText—text START to 678678; TrevorChat—instant messaging at TheTrevorProject .org/Help. It also runs TrevorSpace, an affirming social networking site for LGBTQ youth at TrevorSpace.org.

# REFERENCES

## CHAPTER 1

**The Increase in Mental Health Problems**

American Academy of Pediatrics. 2021. "AAP-AACAP-CHA Declaration of a National Emergency in Child and Adolescent Mental Health." Updated October 19, 2021. aap.org/en/advocacy/child-and-adolescent-healthy-mental-development/aap-aacap-cha-declaration-of-a-national-emergency-in-child-and-adolescent-mental-health.

Bethell, Christina D., Andrew S. Garner, Narangerel Gombojav, Courtney Blackwell, Laurence Heller, and Tamar Mendelson. 2022. "Social and Relational Health Risks and Common Mental Health Problems Among US Children." *Child & Adolescent Psychiatric Clinics* 31 (1): 45–70. doi.org/10.1016/j.chc.2021.08.001.

US Centers for Disease Control and Prevention. 2021. "High School Youth Risk Behaviors Survey: United States 2021 Results." Accessed March 8, 2023. nccd.cdc.gov/youthonline/App/Results.aspx?LID=XX.

US Centers for Disease Control and Prevention. 2023. "Data and Statistics on Children's Mental Health." Accessed March 8, 2023. cdc.gov/childrensmentalhealth/data.html.

US Department of Health and Human Services. 2023. "SAMHSA Announces National Survey on Drug Use and Health (NSDUH) Results Detailing Mental Illness and Substance Use Levels in 2021." January 4, 2023. hhs.gov/about/news/2023/01/04/samhsa-announces-national-survey-drug-use-health-results-detailing-mental-illness-substance-use-levels-2021.html.

## CHAPTER 2

**Peer Counseling Defined**

Walker, Tim. 2019. "Peer Programs Helping Schools, Tackling Anxiety, Depression." *NEA Today*, November 14, 2019. nea.org/advocating-for-change/new-from-nea/peer-programs-helping-schools-tackle-student-depression-anxiety.

**Organizing Support Groups and Clubs**

Bring Change to Mind. bringchange2mind.org/school-programs/high-school-program.

St-Esprit, Meg. 2022. "Teen Helps Start School Mental Health Club After Her Own Loss, Depression." *Pittsburgh City Paper*, January 5, 2022. pghcitypaper.com/news/teen-helps-start-school-mental-health-club-after-her-own-loss-depression-20868310.

## CHAPTER 3

**Peer Counselor Tip: Ethics of Peer Counselors**

National Association of Peer Program Professionals. 2018. "National Association of Peer Program Professionals Code of Ethics for Peer Helpers." *Perspectives in Peer Programs* 28 (1): 18. peerprogramprofessionals.org/uploads/3/4/7/4/34744081/persinpeerprogv28_1_.pdf.


## CHAPTER 4

**Attending Skills—Showing You're Listening**

Hill, Clara E. 2020. *Helping Skills*. Fifth edition. Washington, DC: American Psychological Association: 90.


## CHAPTER 5

**Teaching Skills**

Amen, Daniel G. 2020. "Do You Have an ANT Infestation in Your Head?" Amen Clinics, September 16, 2020. amenclinics.com/blog/do-you-have-an-ant-infestation-in-your-head.


## CHAPTER 6

Becker-Weidman, Emily G., Rachel H. Jacobs, Mark A. Reinecke, Susan G. Silva, and John S. March. 2010. "Social Problem-Solving Among Adolescents Treated for Depression." *Behavior Research and Therapy* 48 (1): 11–18. doi.org/10.1016/j.brat.2009.08.006.

**The Five Steps of Problem-Solving**

Bransford, John D., Robert D. Sherwood, and Tom Sturdevant. 1984. *Teaching Thinking and Problem Solving*. Nashville, TN: Vanderbilt University.

Bransford, John D., and Barry S. Stein. 1993. *The Ideal Problem Solver: A Guide for Improving Thinking, Learning, and Creativity*. New York: W. H. Freeman and Company.

# CHAPTER 7

**Helping People Resolve Conflict**

Sands, Leo. 2022. "Pigs Mediate Barnyard Fights with a Light Touch of the Snout, Study Says." *Washington Post* November 10, 2022. washingtonpost.com/science/2022/11/10/pigs-study-conflict-fight.

# CHAPTER 8

**Suicidal Thoughts and Plans**

Curtin, Sally C. 2020. "State Suicide Rates Among Adolescents and Young Adults Aged 10–24: United States, 2000–2018." *National Vital Statistics Reports* 69: (11).

Hottman, Sara. 2022. "OHSU Reserchers Find Startling Increase in Suicide Attempts by Pre-Teen Children Nationwide." OHSU News, March 15, 2022. news.ohsu.edu/2022/03/16/ohsu-researchers-find-startling-increase-in-suicide-attempts-by-pre-teen-children-nationwide.

Ivey-Stephenson, Asha Z., Zewditu Demissie, Alexander E. Crosby, Deborah M. Stone, and Elizabeth Gaylor, et al. 2020. "Suicidal Ideation and Behaviors Among High School Students—Youth Risk Behavior Survey, United States, 2019." *Morbidity and Mortality Weekly Report Supplements* 69 (1): 47–55. dx.doi.org/10.15585/mmwr.su6901a6.

National Alliance on Mental Illness. n.d. "What You Need to Know About Youth Suicide." NAMI. Accessed May 19, 2023. nami.org/Your-Journey/Kids-Teens-and-Young-Adults/What-You-Need-to-Know-About-Youth-Suicide.

Owen, Quinn. 2022. "Gun Suicide Soars as Cause of Death Among Teens; Rate at Highest Point in 20 Years: Report." ABC News, June 3, 2022. abc7chicago.com/gun-suicides-laws-suicide-rate-guns/11922657.

The Trevor Project. 2022. "2022 National Survey on LGBTQ Youth Mental Health." thetrevorproject.org/survey-2022/assets/static/trevor01_2022survey_final.pdf.

**Homicidal Thoughts and Plans**

Miniño, Arialdi M. 2010. *Mortality Among Teenagers Aged 12–19 Years: United States, 1999–2006*. NCHS Data Brief 37. Hyattsville, MD: National Center for Health Statistics.

# INDEX

code of conduct, for peer counselors, 37–38

cognitive behavioral therapy (CBT), described, 73–74

compassion fatigue, defined, 38

confidentiality, role of in peer counseling, 23

conflict, causes of, 90–91

conflict resolution

    compared to problem-solving, 91

    helping people with, 92–94

    helping with, when only one person is present, 102–103

    and peer mediation, 97

    reflective listening and summarizing in, 96

    resources for, 94, 104

    rules for mediating conflict, 99

    stages of, 97–102

    as teachable skill, 89–104

    what we can learn from pigs about, 94

"Conflict Resolution for Teens: 9 Essential Skills" (Woods), 104

coping skill, mindfulness as, 38–39

Covid-19 pandemic, impacts of, 2, 9, 107

crisis lines and helplines, 107–108, 115, 117, 124–125

cultural differences, importance of awareness about, 48

# D

defining context of the problem, as step #2 in problem-solving, 82–83

Department of Family Services, 115

depression, rate of in kids and teens, 6, 7

discrimination, as source of stress, 9

distracting behaviors, avoidance of, 48

drug use, seeking adult help for teens with, 111–112

# E

eating, importance of eating nutritious and balanced diet, 38

emotional abuse

    defined, 114

    seeking adult help for teens who experience, 113

empathetic, as quality for peer counselor, 30

ENCOURAGES, as acronym to remember attending skills, 48

ethics, of peer counselors, 37–38

exercise, importance of, 38

exploration, as stage in helping, 42–43

exploring possible solutions, as step #3 in problem-solving, 83–85

eye contact, importance of, 46, 48

# F

"Facts for Teens: Conflict Resolution" (National Youth Violence Prevention Resource Center), 104

"fake it 'til you make it," use of, 70–71

feelings

    asking questions to help people clarify theirs, 20, 42–43

    as belonging to an individual, 95

    boys' fear of talking about and expressing of, 9

    cautions with keeping them in, 66

    hurting of, 47, 53, 58, 66, 67, 90, 95, 102

    invalidation of, 58

    journal as place to write about, 71

    reflecting about, 51–53

    responding to big ones, 52

    of sadness or hopelessness (statistic), 7

    validation of, 43

flexible, as quality for peer counselor, 30

food, importance of eating nutritious and balanced diet, 38

## G

Galop (UK), 117

Garey High School (California), peer counseling program, 20

gender role expectations, traditional ones as source of stress, 9

goal setting

in action, 87–88

prompts for, 86

good listener, as quality for peer counselor, 30

Gordoni, Giada, 94

grammatical style or language, importance of matching that of person you're talking with, 48

gratitude journal, use of, 72

guided meditation, as teachable skill, 75

## H

Happier Human website, 70

hate crimes, as source of stress, 9

helping one another

advantages of, 14–16, 18

choosing your helping role, 18

considerations before helping, 29–40

to find solutions, 62–65

formal helping roles, 11–14

how young people can do this, 10–11

setting up helping program in your school, 14

stages of, 42–44

when to seek adult help, 105–119

where you can help, 17

helping program, setting up one in your school, 14

helplines and crisis lines, 107–108, 115, 117, 124–125

*High School Teen Mentoring Activity Book* (Alberta Advanced Education Department), 13

homicidal thoughts and plans, seeking adult help for teens with, 109–111

hope, importance of giving hope, 22–23

humble, as quality for peer counselor, 30

## I

iCall (India), 117

IDEAL, as acronym for problem-solving steps, 81

identifying the problem, as step #1 in problem-solving, 81

I-messages, importance of, 94–95

information, giving of, 65–66

insight, as stage in helping, 42, 43

intolerance, as source of stress, 9

## J

journaling

gratitude journal, 72

as teachable skill, 71–72

## K

kind, as quality for peer counselor, 30

## L

language

importance of matching grammatical style or language of person you're talking with, 48

# U

unhelpful reactions, examples of, 56–58

untwisting thinking, as teachable skill, 72–75

US Centers for Disease Control and Prevention (CDC)

on mental health disorders in kids and teens, 6–7

on teen suicide, 106, 107

Youth Risk Behavior Survey (2021), 7–8, 9

US Department of Health and Human Services, on severe depression in teens, 7

# W

Williams, Brooklyn, 24–25

Woods, Mat, 104

# Y

Youth Engagement Toolkit (Stop Bullying), 17–18, 117

# ABOUT THE AUTHOR

**Dr. James J. Crist** is the clinical director and a staff psychologist at the Child and Family Counseling Center (CFCC) in Woodbridge, Virginia, and a certified substance abuse counselor, working with addictive disorders in teens and adults. At CFCC, he provides psychological testing and individual and family psychotherapy for children, adolescents, and adults, specializing in children with ADHD, depression, and anxiety disorders. He has authored and coauthored numerous books including *What to Do When You're Cranky and Blue*; *What to Do When You're Scared and Worried*; *Siblings: You're Stuck with Each Other, So Stick Together*; *The Survival Guide to Making and Being Friends*; and *What's the Big Deal About Addictions?*

You can visit his website jamesjcrist.com. Or contact him via Free Spirit Publishing at help4kids@tcmpub.com.